CLAWS

CLAWS

Confessions of a Professional Cat Groomer

by Anita Kelsey

JOHN BLAKE

Published by John Blake Publishing Ltd,
3 Bramber Court, 2 Bramber Road,
London W14 9PB, England

www.johnblakebooks.com

www.facebook.com/johnblakebooks
twitter.com/jblakebooks

This edition published in 2017

ISBN: 978 1 78606 285 7

British Library Cataloguing-in-Publication Data:

A catalogue record for this book is available from the British Library.

Design by www.envydesign.co.uk

Printed in Great Britain by CPI Group (UK) Ltd

1 3 5 7 9 10 8 6 4 2

Papers used by John Blake Publishing are natural, recyclable products made from
wood grown in sustainable forests. The manufacturing processes conform to the
environmental regulations of the country of origin.

Permissio͟   ͟ver possible.
All phot   ght. Where
appropria   ͟d to protect
the identi   ͟e to contact
the relevar   ͟e a copyright
que͟   act us.

I would like to dedicate this book to my dearest friend,
Neil Linton, who decided to quietly leave us on
20 January 2008. The hardest, most devastating time of
my life led me to the path I am on now, which is the most
inspiring and joyful. How ironic! God bless you, Neil.
Until we meet again…

CONTENTS

ACKNOWLEDGEMENTS

In no particular order I would like to thank...

David Lowe, my pre-editor. Thank you for your constant support and great work. Fingers crossed for your debut book – it sounds fantastic. Robert Smith, my literary agent, who believed in me and my book from the moment he received the manuscript and has been 100 per cent supportive ever since; my publisher John Blake and all of their lovely staff, in particular my editor, Ciara Lloyd, for her great suggestions, unwavering dedication and constant cheery disposition, and

Ellis Keene, Lizzie Dorney-Kingdom and everyone at Bonnier Publishing for their expert advice; my friends Mohammed Nazam, Emma Southby, Jane Rothery and Marketa Zvelebil, whose encouragement and advice helped me enormously. You are all an inspiration! My university tutor, Keith Buckland, whose support and kindness kept me going throughout my degree course; Svetlana Broussova, a strong teacher, leader, first-class cat groomer and constant inspiration; John Palmer and Alexis Contouris, two friends who gave me constant encouragement on my new path in life; Stacey Ward and Sheryl Wood of the Holistic Cat Groomers Alliance, who are leading the way when it comes to working humanely with cats; my kind-hearted and compassionate sister, Sharon Williams, who is always there – if I could be a fraction of the person you are, I would be content; Dr Andrew Carmichael, Sarah and Wendy Parish at Addison's Veterinary Practice, who have allowed me to work with my most difficult cases at the clinic – your support, knowledge and kindness has been invaluable to me; Chloe Hukin, editor of *Your Cat* magazine, for giving me my first writing break; and the wonderful clients who put their pets in my care (especially the cat owners in this book who gave permission for me to write about their little tinkers and publish photos of them). I can't let the hundreds of cats who have trusted me with their bodies go unmentioned either.

And last, but not least, my long-suffering husband, Gordon, who has to put up with my copious new business and leisure activity ideas every day: you are one in a million and I couldn't have done any of this without you. I hope you can put up with me for many more years to come!

INTRODUCTION

I may as well grow a beard! Every day my face ends up covered in fur, while a few particularly adventurous tufts inevitably gravitate to my nose and ears. To the uninitiated I probably look like a middle-aged woman experiencing an unfortunate reaction to the menopause – but fur's all part of the job for a professional groomer, and while it's hardly glamorous, I think my job is the cat's whiskers.

As a child I remember being asked what I wanted to be when I grew up. My answer was always the same: a singer or to work with cats. As fate would have it I did end up in the music business and was fortunate enough to provide backing vocals for acts including The Spice Girls, Razorlight and Boy George, as well as co-writing and performing lead vocals on numerous dance tracks.

Ten years ago a close friend's suicide prompted me to rethink my life. One evening I was so focused on a recording session that I dismissed one of his calls. He often rang depressed but would soon bounce back, and of course I intended to follow up when I wasn't quite so busy. Sadly he went on to hang himself. My voice crumbled that day – in losing a friend I also lost the fire and passion to sing professionally.

After turning my back on music I embarked on a journey of self-discovery. I am eternally grateful the winding path eventually led to that second dream job, which allows me to work with cats every day, and has delivered a few surprises along the way, including a university degree and the publication of this book.

Cats have always fascinated me. Mum tells me I nagged her relentlessly to walk the longest route to and from school because one particular street in my home town of Mitcham, Surrey, had the most cats sitting outside. This fascination has followed me throughout life, as my husband Gordon can confirm. Every holiday begins with me searching for a cat-friendly destination and ends in tears, as I have to leave my newfound moggy friends behind. Monemvasia in Greece is just one example – it's a cat lover's dream!

I became interested in grooming when, after setting up my successful cat-sitting business, I realised many of my clients' pets were severely matted. There was a general lackof knowledge about coat maintenance and lots of besotted owners were falling for half-hearted kitty growls and abandoning their attempts to get the matts under control. Of course I know that little trick inside out!

Armed with this knowledge I embarked on an intensive five-week course in an animal-grooming salon, based in Ilford, Greater London. From 9am to 6pm, Monday to Saturday, I worked with hundreds of felines, each with different coats and temperaments, and eventually qualified as a cat groomer. Then the second and most difficult phase of training began: dealing with clients and their cats. In time I realised I wanted to tailor an approach to grooming that would take account of each feline's individual background and natural conduct. Every four-legged client became a teacher. Parallel to this I developed an interest in feline behaviour, which I began to study academically. Five years later, I achieved a first-class honours degree in Feline Behaviour and Psychology from Middlesex University – it was the first degree of its kind to be awarded in the UK.

My understanding of cat behaviour defines the groomer I am today. I work holistically and never use face masks, tethers, face hoods or resort to neck scruffing. This has meant thinking outside the box during every single groom.

Working with all kinds of cats and their owners has inevitably led to lots of funny scenarios and even some moving moments. I had a hunch they could form the basis of a book and started to write them down, culminating in this collection of short stories – the first behind-the-scenes account of life as a professional cat groomer.

While the stories are true, the names of my clients

and their areas of residence have been changed to protect their identity. I have also altered some of the cats' names, even though I'm sure most wouldn't mind being mentioned – they are the true stars of the show, after all.

Despite being choked with fur, bitten, scratched, driven to distraction and moved to tears on an almost daily basis, I love what I do and wouldn't change it for the world. I hope you enjoy my confessions. Incidentally, no cats were harmed in the making of this book – only me!

Anita Kelsey

CHAPTER 1

BUDDY, THE KITTY-CAT SHARK

'**I**'m afraid we're going to have to operate immediately. Did you bring an overnight bag?'

Had I heard correctly? An hour earlier I was stuffing my face with a Pret A Manger panini and sipping a latte. Yes, my hand was wrapped in a bandage. Yes, it was throbbing and large as a melon. And yes, I happened to be in A&E – but I was convinced a little ointment or a further injection of antibiotics would see me on my way in no time. In fact, the specialist hand surgeon at Chelsea and Westminster Hospital had just administered a rather blunt, but much-needed reality check. So, how did I manage to end up in this predicament? Let me introduce you to a cat named Buddy…

Affectionately known as 'Kitty Cat' by his owners, Toby and Emma, he is a lovely tabby, who was very nervous about being groomed. I take pride in my holistic work with cats and the low-stress handling techniques I use, so I was confident I could pacify Buddy enough to get his semi-matted coat into tip-top condition without the need for the emergency services. But I was wrong. Why? I'm ashamed to admit it, but on this one occasion, I failed to listen.

It all started so well. I stuck to my usual routine for a potentially difficult groom. Treats? Check. Catnip mouse? Check. Gentle calming strokes on cat's head? Check. But as I progressed to work on Kitty's problem areas (tummy, chest and his nether regions), so began the mighty Rumble in the Jungle. Gradually the intermittent bursts of catty moans turned into a full-blown tantrum. This called for the equipment I introduce to ensure a groom doesn't turn nasty. Towel? Check. Elizabethan collar (a plastic cone used by vets to protect a cat from licking or biting wounds, or chewing at an injury)? Check. Leather arm gaiters? Check. What about plenty of patience? Check. And a deep breath? Check!

As the hours ticked by the air turned blue with catty curses, hisses, paw swipes, growls, attempted bites and a few major struggles. Somehow, I got through the clipping and combing, but the cut revealed the oiliness of Kitty's remaining fur and unsightly flakes of dry skin that resembled dandruff.

After a five-minute breather, during which Kitty wandered casually to his food bowl, I suggested to Toby that we give him a bath. Oh, how I wish those words hadn't left my lips!

Kitty, who thought he had finally got rid of me, was picked up again and placed in the bath, with his head back in the Elizabethan collar as a safety precaution. I began to trickle a few droplets of warm water from my cupped hand onto Kitty's back and as he responded so well, I turned on the showerhead to a light sprinkle. There were a few meows and grumbles, but nothing that suggested to me I should stop – I assumed Kitty would get used to his predicament, let me get on with it, and he would be home and dry in no time.

Wrong!

Kitty's meows became more urgent and in his desperation to escape the bath he was virtually climbing the walls. I quickened the pace, lathering and rinsing as fast as I could, only the damn suds seemed to froth up more and more. As Toby desperately tried to calm him, I was struggling with the never-ending foam and keeping Kitty in the bath. Pleading with him to put up with it for one more minute, I hardly realised that in fact another five had ticked by. In the panic I just wasn't thinking clearly.

Usually, if a cat starts to freak out during the bathing process, the shower is turned off, the cat is helped to relax again, and any remaining shampoo removed as quickly as possible, usually by hand or towel. Seeing that Kitty was now extremely distressed, I took off the collar to try and calm him down.

🐾 Mog Tip: Bathing a Cat

Most cats don't need bathing unless their skin produces too much oil or the skin and fur is particularly dirty or flaky. Both of these conditions will contribute to fur matting. Other factors for needing a bath could be flea control (a bath using medicated shampoo to kill the infestation), the fur accidently getting covered in oil/grease, paint, faeces/urine from another animal such as a fox, or if they need help from their human carer after a stomach upset leading to diarrhoea. Many cats find the bathing process stressful – spending hours afterwards licking their fur to put their own scent back on themselves – so bathing should only be done if necessary and if the cat has the temperament and personality to ensure safe handling.

Correct technique is vital to ensure a quick and successful bath. Make sure your cat is standing on a surface that is non-slip, such as a rubber mat. Introduce the water slowly via a cupped hand or water jug, reassuring them as you go. Just like you would when bathing a baby, always check the temperature of the water first. It should be mildly warm. The sound of the spray from a shower head frightens many cats, unless they are used to being washed from kittenhood, so first try washing your cat in a large sink with a moveable tap – the cat can be easily held in place at the same height as the person washing. A sink also offers sides for the cat to hold onto. Remember to watch for your cat's paws/claws getting caught in the plughole, too!

Speed is essential once your cat responds well to the introduction of the water. Be thorough with the shampoo (it must be safe for cats and unscented. Most pet stores sell shampoos for cats but I like the John Paul brand of pet shampoos and body, ear and eye wipes) , ensuring no suds or water get into the ears or eyes and then quickly rinse with water from specially prepared jugs or from the moveable tap.

Should your cat respond negatively to water, such as panting or fight-or-flight mode, then stop immediately: stress can kill a cat. If in doubt, find a local holistic groomer to assist in helping you bath your cat. In the US there is a Holistic Cat Groomers Alliance (www.holisticcatgroomers.com) but there isn't anything like this in in the UK, unfortunately. But a good place to start is to read the groomers' testimonials online and ensure that the groomer mentions holistic, compassionate and gentle handling on their website. This should ensure you choose your cat groomer wisely.

With this Kitty seized the moment and sank his teeth into my hand with full force. He made me stop and I thank him for that. But I knew I was in trouble: my hand wouldn't move and everything seemed to go into slow motion.

Trying to remain calm, I told Toby to wrap Kitty in a towel and carry him downstairs to be carefully combed so the wet fur would dry unmatted. Meanwhile, Toby's wife, Emma, who had just finished a first aid course the day before, rushed around trying to…

(a) Find her first aid kit
(b) Stem the blood gushing from my hand
    and
(c) Remember how to bandage a hand.

The panic in her voice made us all laugh, relieved to have a distraction. There was a certain irony in passing your first aid exams just twenty-four hours earlier and suddenly forgetting everything the minute there's a patient to work on.

There was nothing else for it: we would have to go

to the A&E at Parkside Hospital in Wimbledon. Sliding into Toby's car, I held my hand up high so as not to drip blood over the smart interior. Kitty had been deposited in the garden to dry off in the sun. What a little sweetheart he looked, a little sweetheart who had taught me an unforgettable lesson!

After waiting for an hour, Toby and I finally walked into the nurse's room, where my hand was thoroughly washed and bandaged and I was given pain relief. Somewhat nonchalantly, the nurse told me to watch out for intense pain or swelling within the next twenty-four hours as this would mean an infection had taken hold and would need urgent medical attention. Then I was dismissed. She had clearly seen it all before – foolish humans not listening to their animals AGAIN! I assured Toby and Emma that I was fine to drive home in my own car and we all cheerily bid farewell. It seemed surreal after such an unexpected and traumatic incident. However, once I started on the journey home I knew I wasn't as okay as I thought. I couldn't use my right hand to drive and had to rely on part of my right elbow and my left hand to steer. It was a stressful drive back. I was exhausted at the end and berated myself for not accepting the offer earlier from Toby to drive me home

When I woke the next day my hand looked like a prize-winning watermelon oozing with green pus. Crazy as it sounds, I didn't understand the implications until I phoned a previous client of mine who was a skin surgeon and whose husband, weirdly enough, had been bitten by their own cat three months before, resulting in a hospital visit. I was told I'd better get it re-checked at the nearest hospital straight away. And I'm glad I did because I have since learned that 95 per cent of cat bites to the hand have the potential of becoming infected. This is due to the fact that millions of bacteria live on cats' teeth, which are like needles and can penetrate right through to the muscle and tendons. Deep within the muscles of the hand, bacteria can take hold before the body has had a chance to fight them.

🐾 Mog Tip: Bacteria And Cat Wounds

This is why cats often develop abscesses after fighting with other cats: because their mouths are full of bacteria. If your cat returns from a night out on the town, nursing a bite wound or deep scratch, it's worth having it checked at your vet's. This will not only give you peace of mind but also ensures any wound is cleaned thoroughly and antibiotics given for a speedy recovery.

It is also important that some annual vaccinations are kept up to date to ensure cats are able to fight infections. International Cat Care has great advice on this and can guide you to the most important vaccinations(www.cats.org.uk/cat-care/key-cat-care/vaccination). It is also advisable to check with your vet regarding what vaccinations are necessary or not for your own personal set of circumstance because indoor cats may not require the same annual vaccinations as a free-roaming mog.

Until the specialist hand surgeon at Chelsea and Westminster mentioned surgery, I had no idea of the seriousness of my predicament. Leaving an infected hand medically unattended could lead to complications such as bacteria travelling from the hand into the arm, which could result, worst-case scenario, in having the arm amputated. There have even been situations where bacteria travelled from the infected hand up the arm and into the heart causing fatalities. Oh, how naïve I was to be happily munching away on my lunch in the A&E waiting room without a care in the world!

Lying there in the ward, I rang my husband, Gordon. I could hear the surprise in his voice as I called to say I wouldn't be home that night. Kitty's owners, after receiving a phone call, were mortified when they heard the news.

The following morning I was prepared for surgery and wheeled into the operating theatre. The nurses seemed somewhat bemused that a domestic cat had managed to maul me to this extent and I felt rather foolish. Counting numbers in my head as the gas mask was put to my face, I thought back to Kitty sat drying in the sun as he watched me being driven from view, smug as you like – how he would love this now.

I couldn't have foreseen it but I spent the next six days in hospital, sharing a room with a Tourette's sufferer, who, weirdly, kept shouting 'Jewish!'. In the end I had two operations to flush the bacteria from the muscles in my right hand and arm. Usually only one is needed, but some bacteria remained in the muscles in my hand after the first procedure, as demonstrated by the green pus still oozing from the wound. During my stay on the hospital ward my entire hand and arm were placed in a heavy-duty cast and held in a brace at an angle to enable the blood to flow more easily.

For breakfast I was given two slices of toast with butter and marmalade on the side. At first, none of the nurses seemed to realise I was incapable of even buttering toast, so I sat for ages staring at the food, with my tummy rumbling. By the time a nurse finally came to assist me, the toast was stone cold and inedible. Luckily my husband saved the day by bringing me breakfast from outside.

Washing and dressing were also a problem. During this period I came to realise just how helpless we are without the use of our hands. The problem is compounded when you lose the use of the more dominant one, in my case the right. Suddenly many things we take for granted become extremely difficult or even impossible to do. Having said this, I'm not one for relaxing and sitting around doing nothing. I didn't feel weak and was still bursting with energy so I armed myself with cat magazines and books on cat behaviour (what else!) and was able to get a good bulk of reading done.

After six days I was sent home wearing a humongous hand brace. This was to ensure I rested the hand so that it could heal. Altogether it took six long weeks and a lot of physiotherapy sessions before I was finally able to return to doing what I love best. During this time

I lost a lot of work. Luckily I have very loyal clients all of whom waited until I was well again, rather than find another cat groomer. I will be forever grateful for that!

While in hospital I had received a lovely bouquet of flowers from Kitty's owners, Toby and Emma, who found it difficult to accept that their sweet cat bit me, causing such damage. I let them know that I would be happy to groom Kitty in the future if they wanted, with one difference... Kitty will not have a bath. And he can talk to me as much as he likes – because next time I'll be listening.

Kitty taught me one of the most important lessons of my career so far and one I shall never forget: always listen to the cat! It's the only way you can work with them humanely.

Mog Tip: A Wee Word About Cat Bites

Cat bites, especially on the hand, must be taken seriously. The first thing to do is to flush out the wound under cool running water to encourage the infection to seep out along with the blood. Squirt with iodine (if you have pets it's a good idea to have some in the home), then wrap your hand in a bandage and go along to your closest A&E. It might be advisable to ask a friend to accompany you or drive you if it's not local.

If your hand starts to swell and hurts badly, even after already being seen by A&E, you need to go back as a matter of urgency. Swelling and pain are signs an infection has taken hold deep within the hand. Also, look out for what are known as 'tracking marks', red lines coming from the wound: this means the infection is spreading. If you see any of the above signs, do not delay, get straight down to A&E.

CHAPTER 2

ORLANDO AND THE INVISIBLE PERFORMING MICE

A pitiful yowl that said, 'Poor old me!' echoed around the room as I set to work on Orlando. For a cat that had reached the ripe old age of twenty, he had certainly lost none of that common catty stubbornness. In fact, as I watched his beautiful red locks fall onto the table, I found myself wondering if flame-haired cats, like their human counterparts, might possess an inherent trait that gives them a fiery no-nonsense attitude.

I first met Orlando two years ago when Sally, his human mummy, called me to groom his frail, matted body. Back then he was eighteen, or indeed eighty-eight in cat years, so perhaps the fact that he was arthritic with high blood pressure, with an over-active thyroid gland, light as a rose petal and deaf as a post shouldn't have been too much of a surprise. What was surprising was that this rather unassuming-looking fellow was in fact no pushover. Within minutes of being lifted carefully onto the grooming table he was crying as loudly as he could, no doubt hoping to convince his mummy that hair removal was actually a form of feline torture.

Orlando was awkward too. One minute he wanted to face right, the next to the left, and then right again. All the while he was trying to nip me with his few remaining teeth. I knew it must have been some time since they last sank into the flesh of a mouse that was unlucky enough to find itself in his path. In fact, Sally had explained to me that in his earlier days, Orlando had been a champion mouser and would return to the house with a rodent several times a week. Now that he was getting on a bit, she said he would sometimes sit there daydreaming, possibly of those days when the spring in his step could land him on top of some poor unsuspecting prey. She said it was as if his gaze was held by the curious sight of a circus of performing mice floating past mid-air, quite out of paw's reach but oh-so tantalising for this particular puss.

It was clear from Orlando's behaviour that evening that the process was going to be long and would need to be executed with some understanding from his point of view. The skin beneath his matted fur was delicate as sugar paper and he hated anything to touch it or his frail little frame. Nor did he want to be held or told what to do. I would need to come up with ways to get around his demands if he wasn't going to get one over on me.

As the evening progressed, the regular breaks for us to de-stress became brainstorming sessions during which I would sip on freshly made coffee and plan my next move. Orlando used these moments to totter about on his arthritic brittle limbs, stopping and intensely staring into space. It was as if that troupe of performing mice had returned to entertain him with their somersaults, perhaps juggling on a unicycle, or even soaring high on the flying trapeze.

Over the years these sessions with Orlando never changed. On a recent visit he was now the grand age of twenty, making him ninety-six in cat years. With his owners going abroad for a month, I decided on a groom that would be a little more dramatic than usual, but would make things easier for all concerned. Also, it was the hottest day of the year, so getting rid of any matting would do Orlando a huge favour: he was going to have his first ever 'Lion Cut'.

This style involves completely shaving off the fur on the cat's body, but leaving the mane and a bit of fur on the end of the tail and legs. Usually I'm a stickler for keeping the result of a groom as natural looking as possible, but there are occasions when drastic times call for drastic measures. Thanks to a little bit of grooming wizardry, a lion cut can resolve the problem of severe matting *and* turn a shy domestic cat into a tiny doppelgänger for the King of the Jungle.

As I entered the kitchen, there in the middle of the room was the ever-shrinking Orlando. His eyes, like hollow glass marbles, watched me bring all of my equipment in before he tottered over to stare at his water bowl. Perhaps those naughty invisible mice were using it to perform a daring high dive!

Seeing Orlando in a world of his own, I couldn't help but smile. There he was, a proud and handsome cat who once ruled the roost. If only he knew the cut he was about to receive – but then at least it would allow his owners to go away without having to worry about all that matted fur.

Perhaps I should have known achieving the lion cut was easier said than done. For the first time, Orlando's human daddy, Robert, was on hand to offer support and empathy to both cat and groomer. Sure enough, Orlando began to pull out all the tricks in the *How to Manipulate Humans Handbook* – he yowled, he struggled, he nipped and he squirmed. I soon realised Robert's resilience was being thoroughly tested.

'I don't know how you do this,' he said, looking at me through a sweat-bathed brow. 'You have the patience of a saint.'

On nearly every angle of Orlando's elderly body there were bones protruding, making it difficult to shave with my clipper blade. If we tried to gently hold him he would start to pant, as if suffering some kind of feline panic attack, and knowing full well, I'm sure, it would make me stop.

When it became clear Orlando would no longer put up with the grooming table, we placed him on the kitchen floor. There I was, reduced to following him around in the sweltering heat, trying to swipe at his fur when an opportune moment arose. Six years of training and hard graft and where had it got me? On the kitchen floor on all fours, trying to groom an infuriatingly single-minded moggy. It was a tad embarrassing, but hey, in this job cats are always showing me up!

After two hours, Robert and I were covered in fur, our throats thick with Orlando's coat. We were both hot, bothered and thoroughly fed up at how badly we had fared at the mercy of a skinny ginger tom. Unfortunately the job still wasn't complete.

Parched from all the activity, I was relieved to enjoy a long-awaited glass of water. As I took a drink, I almost gagged: my mouth was full of fur, and sure enough there were more of Orlando's striking locks floating on the top of my water. I looked over at him and I could swear there was a half-smile fleeting across his chops as he stared into the air around him, perhaps being treated to another amazing acrobatic performance from his imaginary mice.

After an hour and a half, with my back and knees sore from bending down to Orlando's level, I gently scooped him up and carried him out to the garden. Maybe a change of scenery would make all the difference.

I got to work with the clippers and watched as the light breeze carried Orlando's fur to distant lands he no longer explored, far beyond his own garden. For another thirty minutes I battled away, this time tidying certain intimate areas so that Orlando could retain some form of dignity when roaming his ever-decreasing territory.

Finally the job was done, or at least I had finished it as best I could under the circumstances. He had a form of lion cut, or indeed a lion cut for the difficult older gentleman. Not the neatest, but enough to keep Orlando matt-free during the months ahead.

After the grooming session Robert and I sat in the garden, rather amused as we watched a spindly, furless orange creature tottering about. No doubt it would take a while for Orlando to grow accustomed to his striking new look.

Driving home I felt utterly exhausted and was still coughing up furballs hours later. Having done the rounds with Orlando he had won 'paws down'. With his tiny frame, deafness, paucity of teeth and eccentric personality, he had once again sent me packing. I was still none the wiser as to how to make these grooming sessions any quicker.

I do hope the circus of invisible performing mice, which appear to hold Orlando's attention with such ease, will let me in on their secret before next time.

Mog Tip: Grooming Our Ageing Mogs

Elderly cats need a little helping hand with their grooming regime to ensure they remain comfortable and clean. Many suffer from joint problems such as arthritis, which can get in the way of movement, especially when grooming those difficult-to-get-to areas. Always check and trim the claws on a regular basis as these have a tendency to thicken with age and curl over into the paw pads. Some people use human nail clippers, but my advice would be to buy specially designed nail clippers to use on your cat's claws. There are a variety of different styles such as guillotine or scissor-like clippers. I prefer the latter. The internet is full of educational videos showing the correct and safe way to trim a cat's claws.

International Cat Care also has excellent advice and a tutorial video showing the correct method (www.icatcare.org/advice/how-trim-your-cats-claws). Elderly cats' claws need regular human inspections due to less wear and tear from being outside, less climbing or using scratch posts. Also, regular combing of the fur, sometimes combined with using a warm wet cloth, will help keep your elderly cat's fur matt-free and clean. Always ensure you dry with a cloth, too. Pay particular attention to the nether regions as accidents can happen and this area is often overlooked by many ageing mogs. Always start and end any grooming sessions with a tasty treat or cuddle.

CHAPTER 3

PUGILIST PUSS – MY 'ALI' ASBO CAT

The snip, snip of my grooming clippers filled the room as I cautiously set to work on Star, a feisty Himalayan Persian, who certainly lived up to her name. In fact, over the years she has come to remind me of that confident and supremely talented legend of the boxing ring, Muhammad Ali.

Like the world-renowned pugilist, this puss likes to get her own way. Star's diva-like hisses and growls had prevented her owners from maintaining her fluffy white coat for months. However, her demands to cease and desist with any form of grooming meant she barely resembled a cat. The long, thick and matted coat made her look more like a strange hybrid wildebeest that would petrify even the most hardened hunter in the jungle.

Minutes into that first encounter, out of the corner of my eye I caught sight of Paul, Star's human daddy, peering in at the proceedings from the garden outside. Before I arrived he had cleared all the furniture from the living room, as if expecting a home-wrecking ten rounds between Star and her groomer. The look of anticipation on Paul's face made me laugh – it was as if he was standing ringside as Muhammad Ali took on Joe Frazier in the 'Thrilla in Manila', and unfortunately, in his eyes, I was the ill-fated Frazier.

Just as Paul suspected, Star went through the motions, preparing for cat–human combat. However, her manipulative howls and hisses proved useless as any such attempt to intimidate me was met with continued silence.

Next, I carefully placed a towel around Star's shoulders to make a kind of bite-proof bib. With her little face surrounded by fabric she looked very cute and rather puzzled too. When she did go to nip, she got a mouthful of towel.

Ding! Round one to me.

Enraged, she then changed tactics, opting for a move definitely not permitted by the Queensberry Rules – a bunny kick with her hind legs. Those flailing paws had little effect, because I was wearing protective leather arm gaiters. So again it was…

Ding! Round two to me.

Poor Star realised she had pulled too many punches and was no longer top cat. She had no other choice but to stay on the table and allow me to finish off the groom. By the end, perhaps to save whiskered face, she even began to purr and didn't try to jump down. Still, you could tell inside she was smarting. Meanwhile, Paul was jumping for joy at the sight of his beautifully groomed kitty.

As the furniture was returned to the room and Star eventually retreated to her food bowl for some post-match nourishment, the final bell was rung.

Ding! I was the victor… or so I thought.

You see, Star was a very sore loser. Her face was like thunder. She looked very much like a cat with time on her paws for sweet revenge.

As I said my goodbyes to Paul at the front door, I could feel her watching from the stairs opposite, her large eyes burning into my back.

After the first session went so well, Paul assumed all future grooms would be easy. I, however, suspected Star had other plans. Like a boxer beaten with a humiliating blow, she festered dark thoughts, dreaming of a perfectly placed right hook, drawing up a feline plan with genius precision.

And that's just what she did.

A year later, several grooms since we first met in that uncluttered living room, during a moment of complacency on my part, Star bit my arm, following the bite with an impressive left hook that caught my finger. The sharp claws dug deep, sending blood flying all over Paul's lovely white sofa.

Ding! The match went to Star, who clawed back the title with a knockout performance.

A few days later, and with a throbbing swollen finger, I issued Star with her very first ASBO – naturally a novelty one I found online. Paul even framed it and placed it next to a photo of Star. This pugilist puss is a shining example of how a groomer should never be complacent. After all, you can never get one over a cat!

Mog Tip: Dealing with Aggressive Cats During Grooming

This area is never black and white and depends on many factors. For example, has the cat learned that an aggressive response to grooming results in the owner or groomer stopping straight away? Is he or she reacting to a negative grooming experience from the past? Maybe the cat is fearful because the tools and techniques used by the owner cause pain or discomfort when being combed. Does your cat simply not like being touched or held? Each one of these examples requires a different approach. My advice for anyone with a cat who hates the grooming process is to seek advice from a holistic groomer or cat behaviourist. Discover the whys and wherefores regarding your cat's responses and take appropriate action with proper professional advice. This can mean learning how to handle your cat safely and confidently, or training him or her to enjoy being touched and groomed, all the way through to learning which tools are appropriate for your cat's fur type. A professional holistic cat groomer will know how to handle your cat safely and what is the best way to move forward with them in the long term. Education, understanding and patience are all key elements that will ensure even the most difficult cat gets the best treatment plan.

Holistic cat groomers take into account a cat's mind, body and spirit, as well as their natural behaviour, working to ensure the well-being of the animal is met in its entirety. They advocate the practices of no scruffing (holding the cat by the scruff of the neck), no restraints and no face hoods or face masks during grooming.

A cat behaviourist differs from a cat groomer in that they will start investigative work to discover why the cat is being aggressive and when the behaviour started, with the investigation going much deeper. This will typically include taking a full history of the cat's life as well as obtaining a full medical history from the cat's vet. A cat behaviourist will devise a plan of action that is specifically designed to work with a cat's individual set of circumstances and unique personality once the investigative work has been completed. Home visits are usually part of the consultation with a modification plan taking on board not only grooming issues, but looking at ways to improve the cat's environment as a whole. Behaviourists will work with the cat owner and offer continued support in all aspects of the cat's life and well-being. My work as a cat behaviourist and cat groomer is the first of its kind in the UK.

CHAPTER 4

SMOKEY, THE HONG KONG POOEY CAT

At the end of my first groom with Smokey I reeked of pee and poo and couldn't wait to get home to shower, wash my hair and throw my soiled clothes on a burning pyre!

I was introduced to Smokey by his vet, who wanted me to assess his very odd behaviours. He showed strange ticks with his back legs, flicking them out in all directions and particularly when he toileted with number twos. It was the oddest thing I have ever seen. After multiple tests for medical issues turned up nothing by way of explanation, it was down to me to put on my Sherlock Holmes' cap and find out why this stinky chappie was, to put it bluntly, flicking his faeces.

Steve, Smokey's retired owner, met me at the door of his three-bedroom suburban house, looking very much like a man at the end of his tether. With its beautifully-kept garden and chintzy, slightly old-fashioned interior, this was clearly the home of a retiree who was fortunate enough to have had a good job all his life. Naturally he had not envisaged that retirement would ever involve a pet puss who literally flung dung.

Sure enough the smell hit my nostrils as soon as Steve ushered me inside. Everything was covered in plastic sheeting, puppy incontinence pads or towels. The culprit himself seemed entirely nonchalant about the malodorous chaos he was causing in his guardian's home. Stocky Smokey ambled over; elderly and grey, his nose twitching in the centre of his charming moon face – if I didn't know better I would have sworn this was a dignified feline gentleman.

Of course his conduct in the litter tray was anything but gentlemanly. I watched gobsmacked as Smokey performed a bizarre ritual of kicks, twisting and turning with moves fit for a moggy martial arts tournament. Seconds later, he sent a mound of muck flying through the air, which landed with a plop at my feet. I had no idea why he was doing it, but I admit I was strangely impressed.

Out of the firing line, Steve explained that Smokey always had a weird leg tic while toileting and it appeared to have worsened with age. As I'd seen for myself, he looked like he was vying for a black belt in karate.

After a few hours observing Smokey's posture and behaviour, as well as checking around the home for anything that could be influencing his habit, I left totally baffled. In my report for the vet I suggested I could help with Smokey's grooming and hygiene. To be honest, I felt the tic was down to an incurable neurological condition, so even if I couldn't resolve that, at least I could try to alleviate the pong problem.

I commenced the first groom on my table blissfully unaware that no part of me would be beyond the reach of Smokey's doo-doo. The only warning was a shuddering of the legs, followed by an acrobatic high kick, which sent the poop and wee soaring through the air. The fun continued in the bathroom, with Smokey in the tub doing soapy kicks as water and the rest whirled in all directions.

While I was lathering his fur Smokey tried to rip into my hands with his sharp little teeth. There was only one thing for it: an Elizabethan collar that would protect me, but no doubt felt like utter humiliation to Smokey. It certainly wasn't his finest hour. Perhaps sensing his pet's frustration, Steve reached over to try and stroke Smokey's head, knocking my hands towards his nether regions in the process. The response? A squirt of pee, which hit my cheek and was no doubt a bullseye in Smokey's mind.

Back on the grooming table the increasingly grumpy Smokey was quickly blow-dried and gently placed on the floor with one of my catnip mouse toys to play with. I offer catnip mice during grooms as a distraction and at the end of grooms as a nice treat. Most mogs love the smell of this natural herb. He looked very regal with his freshly coiffured fur and seemed to quickly get over the madness of the last two hours.

I still admire Smokey's owner for the compassionate way he cares for his incontinent cat. Despite the difficulties, Steve has persevered when others would have thrown in the towel long ago. As for Smokey, he still gets the odd groom from me, and I like to think he enjoys it now. I've certainly grown to love the old-timer and his excretal eccentricity. Whatever the cause, he's still one healthy, high-kicking cat and has a long way to go before he enters pet paradise, the land many animal guardians call Rainbow Bridge.

[RIP Smokey 5/7/16]

Mog Tip: Odd Behaviours in Cats

Many cats have little quirks that make us laugh, but it's unusual to come across cats with tics and odd behaviours such as I encountered with Smokey. If you see your cat acting out of character (such as staring at the wall for long periods, leaning its head against the wall, head shaking as if something is in the ear cavity or unusual posturing when going to the toilet) your first port of call should be your vet. They'll do tests to look for any neurological diseases or skin conditions. Working with cats that have odd behaviours may include managing their environment. In Smokey's case it was changing the design of his litter trays to low ones, using puppy pads around the home and cleaning him every day in areas he was unable to get to.

Disabled cats or those with odd behaviours are just as loving as able-bodied cats and can live long and happy lives – they just need a little helping hand from us.

CHAPTER 5

MILO'S MATTED UNMENTIONABLES

It was raining cats and dogs when I arrived outside the home of a client with a supposedly aggressive tom called Milo. Sitting behind the wheel of my car, watching the drops of rain hammering the windscreen and literally bouncing off the street, I silently wished I could turn around and go home for an afternoon in front of the TV.

Taking a deep breath, I sprinted for the front door, where a relieved-looking house sitter ushered me in. I had to stifle a chuckle as she explained she was supposed to be keeping Milo's coat in tip-top condition while his owners were away. Milo, however, had other ideas and had scarpered at the first glimpse of her approaching with anything resembling a brush or comb. Worried that the fluffy feline's owners would come home to find their beloved pet looking like he'd just sprouted dreadlocks, the sitter had called in backup – me. I was tasked with sorting out Milo's matted mess before she found herself out of a job.

As usual I was armed with all manner of grooming paraphernalia. My large travel bag on wheels is always packed to bursting with protective leather arm gaiters, heavy-duty gloves, Elizabethan cat collars, catnip mice, toys, electric clippers, combs, scissors, cat shampoos, brushes, plastic gloves and, of course, a large medical bag full of ointments, bandages and plasters to dress human body parts injured by catty claws and teeth. Naturally I hoped I wouldn't be needing them.

I didn't have to wait long to meet Milo, a very pretty young cat with a broad Maine Coon-like face, large green almond-shaped eyes and a long tabby and white coat. This feline heartthrob eyed me suspiciously as he took a sniff of my hand. I eyed him right back, thankful that after our introduction I was able to retrieve my hand unscathed.

As a groomer it's always important to hear what a client has to say about their cat, so I listened intently as Milo's sitter further explained her rather delicate predicament. Entrusted with the care of Milo, she was failing miserably to keep up with the grooming required, particularly when it came to his, ahem, nether regions. The moment anything approached Milo's unmentionables he would lash out, biting and scratching, leaving the poor sitter traumatised and scared to continue. Meanwhile I watched Milo as he climbed into my bag, full of strange smells and torturous-looking objects. He was blissfully unaware of what lay ahead.

Most cats hate to be touched around their privates for obvious reasons: it is a sensitive private area, so it does take some skill on the part of the groomer to negotiate that area. I had a plan for how to deal with Milo, and it began with placing a potent catnip mouse under his nose. Within minutes he had flopped to one side, drooling and writhing, clearly now rather high on the feline-friendly herb some people have dubbed 'kitty crack'.

I donned my protective arm gaiters and the angst-ridden cat sitter looked on, open-mouthed, as I started to trim around Milo's boy bits. She was obviously thinking an attack was imminent. Milo, however, had other things on his mind. In fact, he suddenly started to purr – and rather loudly too. Those striking green eyes shot wide open, as if the strange vibrations of the clippers had awakened something within, something irresistible, which made him forget just how much he hated being groomed.

'I think he's enjoying this a bit too much,' I said to his sitter, who could only respond with a quiet, slightly disturbed giggle.

A cleaner, who had just come into the room with a Hoover in hand, also stopped to watch, intrigued by the change that had come over the combative house cat. The look on her face was priceless. I wasn't sure whether she was on the verge of calling social services, the police or was taking notes for what to try on her own cat back home.

It was surely one of the most bizarre grooms ever. What was supposed to be a difficult encounter with an aggressive mog was actually easy as pie, with three humans marvelling at Milo's rather unexpected behaviour on the grooming table.

After his trim, which was completed without any aggression whatsoever, Milo sat looking rather dazed, or was it satisfied and self-assured? I laughed to think that a difficult groom had, well, a happy ending after all. And I have no doubt Milo is hoping he'll be treated to another trim soon.

🐾 Mog Tip: Entertaining Your Cat

Cats like Milo find all sorts of ways to keep themselves 'entertained', but for the less experimental mog we can rely on good old-fashioned hunting toys to keep even the laziest furbod stimulated. Cats are highly predatory and rod-style toys tap into their natural instinct to hunt and kill. For cats who are kept indoors, or those that had a garden but were moved into a place with no outside access, it is *essential* that they be given lots of stimulation within their own homes, which not only includes toys but also lots of climbing areas.

The best hunting-type toys are those whose attachments mimic a cat's natural prey, such as mice, fluttery bug-type creatures, bird feathers and real fur. The Frenzy Range™ from Purrs In Our Hearts offer around fifty different rod attachments for their Da Bird toy, with the real fur toys ethically and morally sourced. Battery-operated toys such as Undercover Mouse™ can also be great fun, providing independent entertainment at such times when you may be busy. Catnip is also a great safe and fun way for your cat to kick back. The Zebedee™ mice and the Yeowww™ catnip products are fantastic.

Lastly, for some classy cat fun why not try the *Cat Dreams* DVD, with over one hundred different segments of constant action and entertainment? Just check your cat is over a year old or you may need to set up parental control!

For more information, visit:

- www.purrsinourhearts.co.uk/shop
- www.amazon.co.uk/CAT-Dreams-DVD-Movie-Exclusively
- www.zebedeescatnipmice.co.uk

CHAPTER 6

SAMMY, THE SWOONER

I had only just swung my legs out of the car after parking up in a smart cul-de-sac in Putney when a small black-and-white moggy (later found out to be called Mrs Egg) began nudging and curling her tail around them. She appeared to have walked to greet us from the garden of my client's home and even proceeded to guide me and my husband, Gordon, who was assisting me, into the house. It seemed this little minx couldn't wait to introduce us to the cat we'd come to groom.

A friendly young lady named Julia took over from our furry escort and led us into the living room, where Sammy, her huge ginger Maine Coon, sat curled up, looking decidedly unimpressed. He was so much bigger in real life than in the photo I'd received. I watched as his perfect green eyes grew smaller and more intense as he fixed on us like Blofeld's Persian in the James Bond movies – a kind of Sammy death stare.

 **Maine Coons**

Maine Coons are the largest domestic breed of cat. They are the oldest natural breed of cat in North America and named after the area Maine in the USA. The Maine Coon became the official state cat of Maine in 1985 once the feline was introduced there.

Together with the photo, Julia had sent a long email about the problems she was having maintaining Sammy's coat. He hated being groomed with a passion and now sported enough matted fur to keep a family of Eskimos warm for a lifetime. Having been warned of Sammy's strength and seeing just how large he was, I was glad to have my husband there as an extra pair of hands.

When the groom commenced, in Julia's bathroom, Sammy wasted no time in trying to escape. He reared up, swatted, hissed, cried, growled, snarled and tried to bite. It was a tad disconcerting to say the least and both Gordon and I gave each other the silent 'uh oh' look, bracing ourselves for the journey ahead. Every so often Julia would knock cautiously on the door to have a peek at how things were going. I reassured her Sammy's battle cries were normal – they were no more than an attempt to intimidate us the way he had no doubt recently intimidated Mrs Egg, who'd taken such delight in leading us to him.

Cats have a learned behaviour when it comes to antagonistic or aggressive responses. They learn to control a situation to get a desired outcome, and no doubt the best outcome for Sammy was to be placed back in his pod and for Gordon and I to drive off the nearest cliff.

When I'd finished the comb-through and de-matting, I felt confident enough to round off the groom by giving Sammy a bath, which would help to remove even more fur. This was surprisingly uneventful and afterwards I swaddled him in a large comfy bath towel to dry him off.

Just as I lay him on the grooming table my heart skipped a beat. Sammy had suddenly gone limp: he was lying there motionless. Unresponsive. I towelled him as vigorously as I could, trying to motivate him to move and praying he hadn't just lost the last of his nine lives during one of my grooms.

'Come on, Sammy,' I whispered, increasingly desperate. 'There's a sweetie.'

Nothing. I appeared to have a dead cat on my hands.

Damn.

DAMN!

I looked to Gordon, my throat tightening with fear, but he appeared as calm as a vicar eating cucumber sandwiches on a warm summer's day.

'He's fine, just needs a little time to pull himself together,' he chirped.

If ever I've wanted to punch someone in the face for appearing smug and calm while I was flipping out, this was the moment. After counting to ten through gritted teeth, I continued to forcibly dry Sammy, concentrating on his heart area as if performing a particularly frantic cardiac massage.

What words could I possibly use to tell my client her feisty ball of orange fluff was now skipping along the bridge towards Rainbow Heaven? Sweat was dripping down my back and I wanted to cry. Looking at Sammy's lifeless body, I was certain I was now heading for catty hell and a lynching from the client would speed up my entry.

I'm trained in feline first aid, so if the situation had escalated, I would have seen to it that Sammy's sudden swoon didn't spell the end of him.

Then a miracle happened.

Sammy jerked his body and slowly lifted his head upright. I almost yelled, 'You're alive!' but managed to control myself. Instead I rained kisses down on Sammy's head (he was still quite stunned so allowed me this moment) and quickly blow-dried his glossy orange fur, which left him looking as fluffy as a newborn owl.

Calling Julia in to inspect my handiwork, I carefully handed Sammy over like a fragile archaeological treasure. She couldn't believe what I'd done with his stunning coat, nor that he appeared so uncharacteristically calm and serene. Ahem!

Mercifully, feisty Sammy lived to see another day – although I'm not quite sure how his cute companion, Mrs Egg, feels about that.

🐾 Mog Tip: Comfort After a Bathing Session

Now, with several years of experience behind me, I know that sometimes after a bath a cat will appear deflated, as if the wind has been knocked out of them. They will move slowly, as if they feel extremely lethargic, and then spring back to life and start licking themselves. The lethargy is understandable. For some cats water is a shock (the bath is stopped straight away if serious signs of stress are exhibited, such as panting) or the feisty responses can make a cat tire. Frantic self-licking enables a cat to deposit its own smell (from its saliva) back onto itself; it is also how cats comfort themselves.

CHAPTER 7

TILLY TOO TOOS, THE SAUCER-EYED FELINE SCREAM QUEEN

Two large glassy eyes on four fluffy legs confronted me as I entered the room.

The cat had the prettiest peepers I have ever seen, surrounded by a mass of thick golden fur. She was obviously a diva of the highest order, with that luxuriant, if slightly matted pelt to prove it. Indeed glamour puss Tilly Too Toos would give Bette Davis a run for her money, and from the way she looked me up and down, I could tell she didn't think much of me. Now and during the battle of wills that was to ensue, this feline

Bette clearly viewed Yours Truly with nothing but disdain.

Before we met I had an idea of what Tilly would be like. She is a Golden Chinchilla Persian, and my experience of this stunning breed told me to expect supermodel-style looks *and* attitude. Tilly's faithful human servants had warned me of her escalating antics while being groomed, from hissing and screaming to scratching and biting. Yet nothing could have prepared me for the prima donna behaviour that followed.

 **Chinchilla**

The Chinchilla is a breed of Persian with a doll-like face and a variety of coat colours such as gold, silver, blue silver and blue golden. Their coats tend to shimmer because the tips of the fur are a separate colour to the undercoat. Many Chinchilla Persians hate the grooming process due to a dislike of being confined or handled with control taken out of their hands. Sounds like most cats, really!

It was an evening home visit and I had the feeling Jonathan, Tilly's human daddy, knew how things would pan out, but hoped against hope he might be proved wrong. I was met with a warm, enthusiastic handshake and friendly smile before he took me inside, like a gladiator being led to the lions, even though I knew the cat waiting for me was barely a foot tall.

Slowly I began to set up so Tilly could become accustomed to my presence. I could feel those large round eyes checking out the equipment and me as she clambered over everything with indignant curiosity, demanding to know who I was, why I was there and what on earth was in that bag.

After putting on protective leather gaiters, I struck a confident pose behind my table as Jonathan lifted his fiery fur baby towards me. Tilly cowered as I reached out for her to smell my hand by way of introduction, and then let out a frantic scream that took me totally by surprise.

Oh dear! Okay… Hmmm… This was going to be tricky.

Any attempt I made to work on Tilly was met with an Oscar-worthy performance of shaking and screaming.

The scenario played out something like this: I lightly touched her body. She screamed. I stroked her head. She screamed. I placed the clippers on her – without turning them on. She screamed.

I could now understand why Tilly was so badly matted. For years Jonathan had struggled with this difficult behaviour and as her coat became more knotted, he had finally called for backup. I knew then Tilly would have to be shaved – I just had to try and figure out the most humane way of doing it.

Meanwhile her temper tantrum escalated. She was screaming, struggling and trying to bite me as if her life depended on it. It seemed Tilly had made up her mind I was trying to kill her, that the police should be called straight away, and that she should be allowed to resume eating her smoked salmon dinner as soon as conceivably possible. Of course I had other ideas and for two hours Jonathan and I did our best to shave troublesome Tilly without being scratched or bitten. I half-expected a knock at the door from the RSPCA, alerted by concerned neighbours who could hear the cries of woe piercing the air.

Eventually I realised Jonathan was struggling to cope. With each of Tilly's ear-piercing screams he looked crushed, devastated to be putting his little darling through such an ordeal. Tilly was winning and she knew her daddy's resolve was waning. Eyes wide and pleading, she would scream and stare at Jonathan. She seemed to be saying, 'Save me, for God's sake! This woman will be the death of me. *Pleeease!*'

As the caterwauling showed no sign of abating, I realised I needed a plan as much as Jonathan needed a break and Tilly her smoked salmon din-dins. I needed someone who wouldn't be destroyed by staring into those eyes, which seemed to work like kryptonite on a cat lover's heart. Desperate times call for desperate measures, and in this case the solution was my husband. I zoomed off in my car to collect him and we were back to resume the groom within the hour. Jonathan stayed, watching nervously on the side lines.

As I'd hoped, Gordon held Tilly gently but firmly, refusing to fall under the spell of her sorcerous eyes. By 11pm, around four hours after the groom first began, Tilly had received a slightly uneven but perfectly serviceable lion cut. She ran off to help herself to smoked salmon, while we collapsed on Jonathan's sofa, exhausted.

A tiny cat with eyes larger than her head had managed to make me look like a complete beginner. I left deflated and sat up in bed that night, polishing off several chocolate bars while staring into space.

To this day I'm still surprised the knock on the door from the RSPCA never came – not after the shrieks of Tilly Too Toos, the saucer-eyed feline scream queen.

Mog Tip: When Enough is Enough

Cats like to be in control, which is why many dislike being groomed: they do not like to lose that control and be held in place against their will. If escape routes have been taken away, many will try to end the grooming process with warning signs. These can be hisses, low growls, a bat of the paw or even a small half-hearted nip. Most cat owners give up at this stage and in this way the cat learns s/he can control the owner.

If a cat owner has been taught the correct way to groom and what tools to use, they can start to work on their cat's coat in small sections over short periods of time each day. A cat may escalate their dislike by crying more loudly as a way of intimidating the owner to get the desired outcome: for the owner to stop. This also happens between cats ready for a fight. The louder a cat gets, the more intimidating it sounds, with the hope that the weaker cat will heed the warning and back off.

To be confident working with your cat, wear a pair of thick gardening gloves. Ensure you only do five minutes max of combing and then end the session with a tasty treat. Never allow the cat to stop the groom, end the session when you decide. Of course if a cat starts to pant or becomes extremely aggressive or agitated, end the session immediately.

If your cat proves unmanageable then seek professional help from a holistic cat groomer. As I said earlier, an official list of holistic groomers does not exist in the UK, but UK cat groomers will generally advertise whether their work is holistic and compassionate, so ensure testimonials are read and that you ask your chosen groomer about their working methods. It may also be that other avenues have to be explored, such as consulting with a cat behaviourist who deals specifically with grooming issues. Accredited cat behaviourists who work in the field of grooming are rare and so unfortunately I cannot mention any other registered professionals apart from myself within the UK.

I will end this section with the best advice I can give before any grooming issues occur later on in a cat's life. Start early! Get your kitten used to being touched with hands and with a comb or brush. You will reap the rewards when your kitty grows up loving the grooming experience.

CHAPTER 8

TUBBS, THE FAT CAT CAUGHT IN HIS FLAP

At first I thought the fluffy object on the sofa was a soft designer cushion. After all, it was large, round and cuddly and didn't appear to have a face. Suddenly Tubbs looked up and gave a casual stretch. It was a cat! What on earth were they feeding him? Giant deep-fried rodents?

Tubbs, a tabby Maine Coon, who was a little on the heavy side, had truly grown into the name he was given as a svelte kitten by Lily, his young and pretty human mummy. She had taken the day off work to assist with

Tubbs, whose fur was 50 per cent matted due to his weight restricting his ability to groom himself easily, combined with a dislike of being held and combed. Lily had shared various horrendous stories via email about how difficult Tubbs could be, and I could tell she was nervous about getting started.

My first concern was removing the matts, some of which were found in very intimate places. I gave Tubbs my hand to sniff and spent some time playing with him. When he appeared relaxed, I turned on the electric clippers… and suddenly his personality changed.

No longer friendly and playful, he became feisty and vocal. Naturally we tried to pacify the hungry fellow with food, but this didn't last long. In fact he managed to devour several tins of tuna and sachets of Lick-e-Lix cat treats, only to continue with his struggles.

The problem was Tubbs's strength. Being a Maine Coon, the largest of the domestic breed (see also page 56), meant he was no pushover. Like a gladiator he fought and always managed to escape the grooming table, resulting in many a Benny Hill-style chase as

Lily dashed to retrieve him from under the sofa and armchairs.

When most of the matts had been shaved out, Lily asked if I wouldn't mind giving Tubbs a hygiene trim around his nether regions. It was as if she hadn't just witnessed the last two and a half hours of Tubbs trying to rip me to shreds at every opportunity. However, I really wanted to do my best for Lily, who I knew would struggle to maintain Tubbs's most delicate areas on her own.

After a moment trying to think outside the box, I had a flash of inspiration. Tubbs was desperate to go outside to let off steam in his garden. Lily had mentioned the cat flap being too small for him. In fact he had to manoeuvre himself through the flap in order to get to the other side.

'You can open the cat flap now, Lily,' I said with a sly smile.

'Really? Okay then.'

As soon as the flap was opened Tubbs ran to escape and… bingo! He was stuck.

With his head and upper body on the other side of the

flap, I approached his bottom and back legs, which were flailing about in the air. Switching on the clippers, I had him shaved 'downstairs' in no time at all. As he finally disappeared through the flap towards the safety of the garden I thought, *Never underestimate the groomer, Mr T. Not when you're that fat!*

I have since sent Lily a grooming training sheet for her and her partner to work through with Tubbs, along with a diet plan.

Next time I may not be so lucky with a slimmed-down Tubbs, but for now I will enjoy the sweet taste of victory and the amusing memory of his legs wiggling in the air.

Mog Tip: Is Your Cat a Tubbs?

Cats can become overweight very quickly due to many factors, including leaving large amounts of dry biscuits out all day for them to eat, low-quality wet food that contains sugars, giving large portions of food with each feeding session, and lack of exercise (especially indoor cats with a lack of stimulation or toys). Top tips for keeping your cat healthy include:

(a) Understanding the correct amount of food your cat requires depends on the typical healthy weight of his or her breed and age. To determine this, speak to your vet and then weigh out portions to the correct amount.

(b) Get the balance right between wet and dry food portions. Giving wet and dry food can mean your cat is getting two meals in one sitting, so reduce the amount between them to ensure both equal one meal portion only.

(c) Ensure your cat has good-quality wet food, with their kibble served separately and placed in feeding puzzles to stimulate hunting and foraging. Feeding puzzles are gadgets or devices that encourage a cat to work out how to get the food placed inside it out to eat. A great source of information on these and where to buy or how to make them can be found here: www.foodpuzzlesforcats.com/

(d) Encourage activities such as play sessions with hunting toys as well as tall climbers for them to jump on.

(e) Don't give in to your cat's constant cries and demands for food throughout the day. Your attention leads to a cat forming a habit because it knows crying reaps the ultimate reward: YOUR LOVE AND ATTENTION.

CHAPTER 9

DENZEL, THE COPYCAT CAT

Not all of my stories centre round the furry critters I groom. I have met some, ahem, very interesting owners too. Felicity, who was the guardian of a gorgeous Norwegian Forest cat called Denzel, was especially memorable... Perhaps not for the right reasons.

Felicity was a woman who always seemed to get what she wanted when she wanted it. She was wealthy enough to have a 'service book' in which she listed the numbers of her housekeepers, gardener and even financial advisor, and when she felt her darling feline was getting too scruffy, the groomer. This, of course, was me.

My first encounter with Felicity was uncomfortable. She had told me her cat was nervous and didn't like being groomed. When I saw Denzel's coat was brittle and balding in places I suspected the usual culprits of poor diet, health or stress. After discussing this with Felicity, I sensed it was the latter, yet there was no obvious reason why Denzel should be such a stress-puss. His home was extremely spacious and comfortable and he appeared to have an owner who catered to his every whim.

Only when I started the groom did I find the root of the problem – Felicity.

I began with Denzel lying calmly on the grooming table and his owner fidgeting nervously beside me.

'Poor Denzel,' she said, as if she had abandoned the perfectly happy chappy I had before me to a dreadful fate.

'He's fine,' I insisted in my best deadpan voice while giving his head a good stroke.

Next, I got out my comb and lifted a section of fur.

Denzel meowed, completely normally, more to register my presence, as is standard for any moggy during a groom. I looked over at Felicity, whose eyes were now welling with tears.

'I can't bear it! He's going to hate it,' she said, her voice wavering.

I assured her it was okay and got on with grooming, but the more anxious and neurotic Felicity became, the more little Denzel began to mirror her behaviour.

Next, her phone rang and she started to have a heated argument with another of her 'service providers' right next to the grooming table. Clearly sensing the harshness in her voice and demeanour, Denzel began to hiss and play up in a classic feline response to negative human energy – cats have an amazing ability to pick up on nervous, erratic or brash behaviour.

With Denzel worsening, Felicity the worry bucket became jumpier than ever but when twenty long minutes had gone by, I'd had enough. After downing tools I bravely explained that her energy was contributing to her cat's fear of being groomed. Bracing myself for how she would react, I then asked if she would leave the house while I completed the job. Usually I like owners to be present, but on this one occasion I felt her absence would make a world of difference.

At first Felicity looked stunned that I had the audacity to ask. However, she did leave, albeit with a smirk and a bit of a chip on her shoulder.

The rest of the groom was a breeze: Denzel immediately calmed down, helped by the classical music I put on. He actually became quite a sweetie. On her return Felicity was delighted with how smart Denzel looked and I was booked to groom him once a month.

I always dreaded that drive to her house, my heart sinking as each mile brought me closer.

Perhaps the eventual outcome was inevitable.

I arrived for the usual monthly appointment and unloaded my equipment into Felicity's apartment. I'd been driving around for twenty minutes looking for somewhere to park without any luck, so I'd left the car at the side of the road, intending to check with Felicity if it would lead to a parking fine, but her response was far from clear and I could tell she was getting irate. All I wanted was a straight answer about whether I could face a £65 penalty, or even worse, have my car towed.

'Is there something wrong with you?' she asked in a patronising voice, pointing to her head.

I could feel my heart beat faster and the blood begin to rise but I tried to keep my cool.

'You don't need to be rude,' I spluttered.

Again, she pointed to her head.

'I'm not being rude, but are you stupid or something?'

That was it: the moment had arrived, the moment I could finally stand tall and declare I would no longer work for her.

'I'm done,' I said. 'Find yourself another groomer, I'm leaving.'

Felicity looked stunned. Probably no one had ever spoken to her like that before.

After picking up my table, I walked to my car, painfully aware the rest of my belongings were inside and I hated confrontations. *Oh no!*

I was walking back to the apartment when Felicity came running at me like a bull with its backside on fire. In fact, she might even have had steam coming out of her nostrils. I nearly had a heart attack and stopped in my tracks as she blocked my path, screaming at the top of her voice.

'How *dare* you speak to me like this! Are you mental or something?'

Somehow I remained polite and in the end managed to shift her to one side. I half-expected her to produce an axe and run at me in a re-enactment of a bloody battle scene from *Braveheart*. Then it all went quiet. I had no idea where Felicity had gone, but I collected the rest of my things in silence, watched by my feline friend, Denzel. Of course he was not at fault and my heart sank as I knew this would be my last sight of him.

Back in the car I was fumbling with the keys to make a swift getaway when Felicity reappeared, her face etched with the look of a crazed wildebeest. It was like that age-old scene from a horror movie, where the driver can't get the key in the ignition and the baddie is fast approaching.

The engine started and I locked the doors. Just as I was about to move off, Felicity made an unexpected move, landing with her arms outstretched on the car bonnet.

She held fast as I slowly reversed, my mind racing as I asked myself, *Oh dear, what the hell do I do now?*

Thankfully she let go, and took up a position in the middle of the street, still screaming profanities for all she was worth.

I manoeuvred the car around her and, safely past, put my foot down. Minutes later, I had to pull over for a few deep breaths to calm myself.

I loved Denzel and I do miss him, but I wouldn't go back to Felicity's for all the tea in China. She really is what they call a Crazy Cat Lady.

Mog Tip: Creating a Stress-free Environment When Grooming Your Cat

Cats are sensitive creatures and pick up on any tensions or stress a human may be carrying so it's best to approach your cat for a groom when you are feeling relaxed and in a good headspace. Ensure the room you groom your cat in is quiet and free from any loud noises. A really good source of music to create a peaceful atmosphere is *Music for Cats* by David Teie, put together after extensive research on cats and frequencies, resulting in beautiful sounds mixed with cat purrs and the sound of kittens suckling on their mother's teat.

Praise your cat with a gentle soft voice and use treats and toys to give the experience a positive association. Allow him or her to move freely within your grasp, working with the areas your cat presents to you. Get this right and you will have a very relaxed, contented kitty on the grooming table.

CHAPTER 10

HARRY, THE FOUR-PAWED ASSASSIN

The email didn't bode well. Harry was a large, white six-year-old Chinchilla Persian, who hated being groomed. His thick coat had become matted all over and his owner, Jackie, was at a loss as to what to do. She wondered if I might be able to help.

To be frank, I wasn't sure. As I've mentioned earlier, this stunning breed is known for its skittish diva-like antics and many Chinchilla Persians have an extreme hatred of grooming. Still, I was touched by Jackie's honest cry for help, and found myself parking up behind her flat, trying to ignore the alarm bells ringing in my ears. I left my equipment in the car, feeling somewhat doubtful I would need it, and went to meet my potential client.

Harry was not pleased to see me. When I took a step towards him, he flew across the living room, paws and teeth at the ready, clearly poised to launch an attack. Thankfully I was able to grab the nearest cushion to protect myself, and used another one to usher him out into the corridor. I wasn't expecting such immediate aggression, but Jackie was quick to defend her sweet Harry.

'I don't know why he acts the way he does. With me he is so nice.'

Of course there is always a reason for such behaviour and Jackie explained Harry had had a bad start in life. She got him as a rescue cat and was informed he had suffered cruelty from previous owners.

Harry's aversion to being groomed appeared to have started after two trips to a dog-grooming parlour. I have seen this many times before in cats who exhibit severe aggression towards being groomed. No matter whether the handler did everything correctly or not, Harry's perception of the experience was negative. Now it was deeply rooted in his memory and nothing was going to change this moggy's mind.

I knew then that Harry's matts couldn't be sorted on a quick home visit without serious risk of injury to me and psychological trauma to him. There was only one way forward: Harry's groom would need to be completed under sedation. I made my escape, with Harry shut in Jackie's bedroom, and then called my friend and colleague, Andrew.

Andrew is my local vet and runs a small, personalised practice in West London. (In the reception area, besides the usual pet products he sells olive oil from his grove in Crete and freshly laid eggs from his chickens here in the UK.) I'm lucky that he makes the practice available to me when sedation is required for a groom.

The day of Harry's appointment came and I was in the waiting room when Jackie carried in a cage that was rattling furiously and from which I could hear hissing and spitting. When Andrew performed the health check required ahead of sedation he had never seen anything like it: Harry appeared to have regressed to a feral state. Opening the carrier would be a death wish. That's when I remembered my trusty leather gloves and arm gaiters. Despite Andrew's apprehension, we agreed I would wear them to hold Harry still while he performed the sedative injection.

The roof of the carrier opened and when I grabbed Harry, he squealed and writhed in horror. Anyone would think we were performing an amputation without anaesthetic. I was counting the seconds and, although Andrew was quick with the sedation needle, it still felt like time had frozen and the moment was never going to end.

Mission accomplished, we waited for the sedative to do its work. Yet fifteen minutes later, Harry was still hissing and his almond eyes were wide open.

Intrigued, Andrew re-checked the dosage. Although it had been correct, we decided on a top-up. Harry wasn't quite so highly strung for the second injection and afterwards we covered the carrier with a blanket and put him in a quiet room.

Ten minutes later, I checked on him. His eyes, rather

than being tightly shut as he dreamed of chasing mice and rabbits, were fully open. Harry stared out at me, defiant and wide awake. He was so angry and charged up that the sedative still wasn't working.

Andrew agreed to a second top-up of sedative, Harry's third injection, and eventually, an hour after we had started, the highly strung bundle of fur fell asleep. Or so we thought.

I was happily clipping the last of Harry's matts when, without warning, he awoke with a deep growl. While he didn't have the strength of a fully functioning cat, he tried to bat me with those sharp Persian claws. Andrew and his colleagues had never seen anything like it. At this stage Harry could not be injected with more sedatives, so only by using sleeping gas could I get to the end of the groom – I guess extreme cats call for extreme measures.

After a few breaths of gas Harry started slumbering again, leaving me free to shave the unsightly matts around his lower tummy and bottom and lastly, clip his nails.

With the groom finally over, Harry was given a

reverse sedative and placed in his carrier with a nice warm blanket. As he came to, he looked so sweet and vulnerable that I wanted to reach in and stroke him until Jackie arrived to pick him up. Tempting as it was, I'm sure it would have resulted in a nasty bite.

Later that evening, when he was back home, Harry chomped his way through a dinner of freshly roasted duck and, according to Jackie, was his usual sweet self again.

I did provide Jackie with a training sheet to try and counter Harry's aggressive response to being groomed, but nothing worked. Three years on, he still has his matts removed under sedation.

Harry the four-pawed assassin clearly has a bone to pick with the world. Although surely his prime target, I'm thankful my bones are intact!

🐾 Mog Tip: Working with Abused Cats and Rescue Cats

Cats that show signs of abuse, or have been rescued and are known to have had an abusive past need plenty of patience and understanding. They need time to acclimatise to new situations, so always provide lots of safe spaces and hidey-holes, gently working with them using food. Allow them to set the pace when it comes to how much interaction they are ready for, although after a certain amount of time a kitty may be gently challenged out of his or her comfort zone, again using their favourite food or toys. Every cat's story and personality is different, but time and patience, as well as seeing life from a feline's point of view, will usually see improvements before long. Many abused rescue cats have transformed beyond recognition with love and understanding to become the most affectionate and loyal moggies an owner could wish for.

CHAPTER 11

DUCHESS OF WALTHAMSTOW

Duchess shifted on the table, trying to get comfortable without success. She let out a pitiful mewl, a sign she was in pain and in fact the only clue that the mass of matts before me was actually a cat. With her coat dangerously knotted from chin to tail, Duchess, a three-year-old white Chinchilla Persian, was the worst case of matting I have ever seen.

I am fortunate that I rarely have to face the consequences of animal cruelty. The cats I deal with have responsible owners who give them the love and care they deserve. Until she landed on my table for her much-needed sedation groom, Duchess's life had been so very different. Mercifully that was all about to change, thanks to her heroic new owner.

Toying with the idea of getting a cat, Philip, a young single estate agent, was looking at a website when an advert with a photo of a large white ball of fluff caught his eye. The post requested urgent new owners for what seemed to be an unwanted pet. As luck would have it, Philip had thought about getting a Persian. Once again he looked at the picture of Duchess.

He would have to move fast if he was to become a cat daddy after all.

After quickly replying to the advert, Philip was surprised to receive an immediate response, suggesting a visit that very evening. Luckily the owner was based nearby, so a somewhat dubious Philip agreed to visit only a few hours later.

When Duchess was presented to him, she was barely recognisable. That big, bouncy bundle of fur in the photograph was in dreadfully poor condition. Realising this was a cat who needed to be properly looked after,

Philip made the snap decision to take Duchess with him and give her a better life. But Duchess's new beginning didn't happen straight away. When Philip tried to stroke and comfort her that night she cried and hissed, a consequence of how sore and tender she felt underneath all that matting.

Desperate to ease her suffering he emailed me, detailing the whole sorry tale, and we agreed to have Duchess groomed under sedation to restore her to her former regal self.

There on the vet's table, poor Duchess looked like life couldn't get any worse. Philip had brought her all the way from East London in a pet carrier on the Underground, a journey that would unnerve even the most robust of cats. Not only that, but Duchess's matts were so advanced, they were now what we groomers call 'pelts'. These occur when the knots are left for such a long period that they clump together, become hard and tight, and weigh down the cat's body and skin. It is not uncommon to find sores and even serious diseases like skin cancer when the pelts have been removed. I knew I had to get started straight away.

CLAWS

Philip tenderly kissed Duchess on the head before she received her sedation injection and drifted off to sleep. Only when she was slumbering deeply did he leave her side.

I started on her neck and jawline and almost immediately got more than I bargained for. As the clumps of carpet-like fur fell away, they revealed a lump on her chin that didn't look right. I called Andrew the vet over and after squeezing the mass between thumb and forefinger he could tell it was a pellet from an air gun. As if her snarled coat wasn't bad enough, poor Duchess had been shot at and her skin had healed over the plastic bullet, leaving it embedded. As it was fairly deep and unlikely to do harm, the vet advised against surgery. Duchess would shortly wake up completely bald, and giving her unsightly stitches in the face on top of that seemed a step too far.

The groom took an extremely long time due to Duchess's fur and skin being virtually indistinguishable. I was determined not to nick her with the clipper blades. After everything she had been through, Duchess deserved to be left unblemished.

Left: Buddy, the kitty-cat shark.

Right: Orlando having a rest during a grooming session.

Below: Star, my 'Ali' ASBO cat, greeting me upon my arrival.

Smokey, sitting on an incontinence pad.

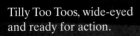
Tilly Too Toos, wide-eyed and ready for action.

Above: Milo after his groom.

Right: Harry, pre-pounce!

Above: The Duchess sporting her new lion cut.

Left: Minou and his adored brother Binty.

Below: Minou and baby Zina twenty-four hours after first meeting.

Right: Little Wolf after his wash and blow-dry.

Below: Lucky on the day she was rescued.

Left: Lucky relaxing at home after her groom.

Below: Frank, the reverse kick-the-cat cat!

Boyd, the old tart.

After a few hours the groom was completed without any unfortunate cuts and Duchess was given a reverse sedative, then placed gently in her carrier and covered with a blanket to keep her warm.

When she awoke she started to shiver uncontrollably, a common response in cats waking from sedation or anaesthetic (the shaking is a side effect of the chemicals used in veterinary anaesthesia that disrupts the temperature control centre of your cat's brain temporarily). No doubt Duchess was also feeling rather chilly minus the thick woven carpet of fur that had enrobed her body for so long. I reached in and tucked the blanket around her, then gave her face and head a reassuring stroke. Despite all her trauma, Duchess filled the room with some of the loudest and most satisfying purrs I have ever heard.

Philip was understandably shocked about the air-gun pellet. I asked if he wanted to report the owners to the RSPCA, but he wasn't keen – we didn't know for sure it was them who had shot Duchess. Philip just wanted to get her home and give her the royal treatment that all proud-as-peacock Persians love.

Later that evening I received a lovely email from Philip with a photo of Duchess eating her evening meal. She looked so tiny with her hairless body and cute little head sporting the few white tufts of fur I was able to save.

Within six months Duchess had grown a beautiful, matt-free coat and now she loves the regular brushing sessions she gets from Philip.

I'm in awe of Philip for rescuing a cat found in the most dreadful condition, and Duchess for maintaining the sweetest little personality, despite everything she went through during her first three years.

Hats off to them both!

Mog Tip: Dealing with Concern for a Cat

If you spot a cat that looks in poor condition, or you are slightly concerned by its weight or movements, please call the animal welfare society in your country. In the UK this is the Royal Society for the Prevention of Cruelty to Animals (RSPCA: www.rspca.org.uk). Alternatively, contact your local animal rescue centre. The RSPCA and most animal rescue centres have specially trained animal welfare officers who will take your details in confidence and investigate any concerns as a matter of priority.

CHAPTER 12

MINOU'S MISSING MOJO

I've received many notable grooming requests in my day, but none quite as shocking as that from a lovely middle-aged cat owner named Derek. He had experienced perhaps the most devastating way to lose a pet, and did not hold back on the registration form I give out to all of my clients. Binty, one of his ginger moggies, had been murdered.

This tragic and violent death had left Binty's brother, Minou, so upset that he was failing to groom properly. Derek needed professional assistance to ensure his beloved cat's coat remained in a hygienic condition, and he also hoped a bit of pampering and TLC might return Minou to his loving, energetic self.

In happier times the two cats were inseparable. Derek described them as 'best of friends' and reminisced about all the mischief they would get up to. They could spend hours sitting side by side in an open window; sniffing the breeze and watching birds go to and fro. Knowing their mischievous personalities, Derek was glad neither of them had ever hurt a bird or carried an injured mouse into his tiny flat as a present.

Sadly Derek lived next to a man who hated cats with a vengeance. He would complain about Minou and Binty even though he didn't have a garden where they might have dug up the odd flower, as cats are prone to do. The neighbour's front door wasn't even beside Derek's, and thus he would rarely have been confronted by the two friendly felines scampering home for dinner. Yet over time the complaints about Minou and Binty became more frequent and increasingly sinister. While he knew they thrived in the great outdoors, Derek started to worry about his cats' safety each time they left the flat.

Then one night Derek returned home to be confronted by his worst nightmare: Minou and Binty were lying lifeless side by side on the doormat. They each had terrible head injuries. Only when cradling them did Derek realise Binty had already passed away beside his brother, but for Minou there was hope: he was still breathing, ever so slightly.

The animal hospital that received the cats told Derek their heads had been smashed together with considerable force. This was most likely done by a human. Although the RSCPA was informed and interviewed Derek's neighbour as the chief suspect, there was no proof of his involvement. Naturally Derek was devastated no one would be brought to justice, but he made the wise decision not to be eaten up with thoughts of bitterness, anger or revenge. Instead he would pour his energies into helping Minou recover, as well as help himself remain living in a place he had called home for so long.

After many months of operations, the plucky puss began to pull through. Minou's health improved and he started to put on weight. Yet he wasn't quite the same: the zest for life he'd shown in the company of his beloved brother had gone. Once a happy-go-lucky, fun-to-be-around mog, Minou now lay depressed in his bed, pining for the sibling that could never be brought back. With his lifelong companion gone, Minou had lost his mojo.

Derek didn't know what to do. Having confined his cat to a life indoors for his own safety, he watched as Minou's spirit faded. When he realised Minou was beginning to smell of urine due to a lack of grooming, Derek contacted me to see if I could help with a professional pampering. Shocked to the core over the reason behind Minou's heavy heart, I promised to do all I could.

Over the years I've discovered one of the most useful items in my bag is a simple catnip mouse. When I first saw Minou, a listless ball of orange fur staring up at me from his bed, I did wonder if anything would perk him up. He was so quiet and unassuming, disinterested in life in general. Thankfully this changed when I sat down gently beside him to make him feel comfortable and produced his pungent little present, a catnip mouse. After a whiff of what I call 'kitty crack', Minou flopped on the floor, writhing in pleasure and obviously having the most fun he'd had in months.

On the grooming table Minou's mood darkened again. He didn't need to be shaved, but a thorough comb-through was required. While Derek fed him his favourite tuna flakes to distract him, I combed his lovely orange fur. Near his back end the stench of urine was particularly strong, so I wasn't going to leave without giving him a bath.

Ten minutes later, after a relatively calm bathing session, Minou was lifted from the kitchen sink dripping wet. He didn't like the sound a hairdryer made, so we wrapped him in a warm towel and placed him in his bed by the radiator: he was fresh, content and clearly loved being pampered.

Although I gave Derek lots of advice about toys to encourage Minou to play, he remained concerned about the future. This was a cat that loved company, but his owner couldn't be with him twenty-four hours a day like Binty had been. I wished Derek all the best and made sure he had my number in case there was anything else I could do.

CLAWS

A few days later Derek emailed me with an idea. He had been watching a programme about a cat rescue centre and wondered if getting a rescue kitten as a playmate for Minou might help. At first I was cautious. As a behaviourist I have seen many households where well-meaning owners introduce a second cat, supposedly as a friend, only for the two mogs to clash and resort to a life of tolerating each other.

After mulling things over Derek came up with a solution: if Minou or the kitten reacted badly to their new companion, Derek's sister, Francis, would take the kitten.

A few months passed and I didn't hear from Derek. Then I received a photo on Facebook that brought tears to my eyes: it was Minou contently stretched out on Derek's bed with a tiny sleeping kitten nestled into his belly.

Baby Zina had been rescued from the streets and, after such a tough start in life, had settled well into Derek's flat. Minou took to her immediately, washing her tiny body and becoming like a protective older brother.

I have since received more photos of the two cuddling,

Baby Zina clambering over her friend's body and the two of them playing with a feather chase toy. It seems almost too good to be true.

Of course nothing can bring back Binty, but I am overjoyed Minou has turned a corner and can enjoy a happy life once again.

Thanks to Baby Zina and Derek, Minou's finally got his mojo back.

🐾 Mog Tip: Grieving Cats

Not much is known about how cats grieve, although one can assume that a cat would be affected by the sudden disappearance of a constant in their life such as another companion cat or a loving owner. Grief or anxiety in a cat can take hold in many different forms and can sometimes be so subtle that an owner will not notice what is happening. Sarah Heath, who runs the cat blog, Messy Beasts, has researched and written in great depth about grief in cats. She states: 'Humans understand grief as being the sense of loss following a death. It is a form of anxiety felt at the abrupt severing of a relationship or the sudden absence of a familiar person or animal companion. Cats react to the sudden absence and, therefore, may show anxiety or grief in situations where death is not a factor. Grieving may be related to the death or sudden absence of a human companion, caregiver or animal companion.'

Some cats may show signs of grieving or anxiety by sleeping more than usual, over-grooming or lack of interest in food or human interactions. Whatever the signs, owners must take into account that their cat may be affected by death and could be showing signs of grief. Extra TLC and patience can help, as well as extra attention and play sessions. Don't assume that because your cat is an animal it will not be affected by the death of a companion cat or even our own emotional state. Keep an eye out for changes in usual behaviour and act quickly.

More information on cats and grieving can be found on messybeast.com/cat-grief, where Sarah Heath covers many angles on this subject matter – it's a truly fascinating read.

CHAPTER 13

I'M FARTAPUSS

From scratching and biting to heart-rending mewls, cats who don't like being groomed will resort to anything to try and escape being clipped – even if it's essential for their health and well-being. I thought I'd experienced all the tricks in the book, until I met an enterprising Siberian Forest cat called Eric. Let's just say his memorable method easily trumped all the others I've come across.

When I was first introduced to Eric he seemed a perfect gentleman, stretched out by a roaring fire and looking for all the world like butter wouldn't melt in his mouth. He lived with his feline friend Wiggo, and human parents, Christine and William, by the edge of the Thames in pretty Barnes, south-west London. Eric's beautifully fluffy silver and white coat was matted, and although Christine had told me both cats could be a little nervous, I expected this would be a relatively straightforward booking.

Shortly after the introduction it dawned on me that Christine, who had just come back from work, was still wearing her smart black office clothes. As I would need her assistance I asked her to change, and after making me a nice cup of tea she disappeared upstairs. When she came back in floaty pyjamas I had a chuckle to myself. If Eric did prove a challenge, she wasn't exactly kitted out in the robust jumper and jeans that I usually wear for a bit of extra protection from scratches and bites.

But back to Eric. I placed him on the grooming table and was pleased that he didn't react aggressively. As I got to work with the clippers he began low catty murmurs that Christine admitted had been menacing enough to make her stop grooming him in the past. When he realised the same tactic wasn't going to work this time, Eric's vocalisations became louder and more desperate. He was doing everything in his power to intimidate me. I could swear I saw Wiggo, who had taken his place at the fire and whose coat was in better condition, smirking as he stretched out, looking so very relaxed.

For Eric the last straw came when I tried to deal with the larger matts on his undercarriage. He started struggling and we decided to take a break, during which Christine ran to the kitchen for cat treats; he practically got his head stuck in the jar.

When we resumed Eric was not a happy camper. He started to growl and the effort it took to control him, together with the heat of the fire, soon had sweat pouring down my back. By this stage Christine's husband, William, had also come in from work and was enjoying the spectacle of Eric being clipped from the comfort of the sofa. As Christine and I struggled valiantly on, William's smart comments like, 'It's all my wife's fault, she never grooms them', really didn't help – I could see Christine growing as exasperated with the big man on the sofa as I was with the little man on my table.

Desperate times call for desperate measures, and as Eric's behaviour deteriorated further, it meant giving him his favourite treat, ice cream. Christine put a scoop in a dish and placed it on the table. Within two minutes Eric had lapped the lot. He looked even more distraught, though when I recommenced the groom, filling the bag hanging from the table with yet more fur.

As Eric got smaller and smaller, the air suddenly turned foul. I tried to politely ignore the stink emanating from his nether region but Christine turned away, gasping for breath.

'It's time we took a break,' she announced. 'I need a drink. He's started farting.'

When we eventually got back to work, the last half hour of the groom was a decidedly smelly affair, with Eric's ill wind filling the room. The silent but deadlies were fired in all directions as a last act of defiance, clearly in the hope it would bring an end to what he saw as a humiliating ordeal but was in fact essential to improve the state of his matted coat.

The regularity was astounding. It was as if Eric had saved a year's supply of windy weapons just for this moment. In the face of his farting, Christine and I battled on regardless, grimacing with creased noses and narrow eyes. Finally we finished and a smaller, much-less-furry Eric was placed on the floor, where he lay down, proud as punch. No doubt he assumed his blitz of backdoor bombs had forced a truce.

Poor Christine, mortified that I had to work through an attack of feline flatulence, spent the next ten minutes apologising as I packed my things away. In fact I was rather impressed: Eric had taken a creative approach to halting his groom that had been not only an eye-opening experience, but also an eye-watering one.

After leaving the house I sat in the car and quickly texted my husband: 'Run a bath for me, I've just groomed Fartapuss'.

The next time I see Eric, I'm taking a gas mask!

🐾 Mog Tip: Flatulence in Cats

Do you have a gassy mog? A smelly, methane-ridden little terror? No? Guess it's just me, then!

Flatulence is defined as excess gas in a cat's stomach or intestines. It is more common in dogs than cats, but cats can develop gas when food ferments in the digestive tract, when they swallow air after eating too fast or too much, or if there's a disorder of the stomach, small intestine or colon.

A little gas is a natural part of the digestive process and usually passes quickly. Excessive gas, however, especially when foul smelling and accompanied by other symptoms, including the following:

- Pain when you touch your cat's belly
- Bloated abdomen
- Decreased appetite

- Vomiting
- Diarrhea
- Excessive drooling
- Scooting across the floor
- Bloody bowel movements

These symptoms may indicate that something is wrong in your cat's digestive system.

So What Are the Causes of Flatulence in Cats? The following are some common causes of feline flatulence:

- Diets high in wheat, corn, soybeans or fibre
- Dairy products
- Spoiled/old food that has been left out for too long or is out of date
- Overeating
- Food allergies
- Poor food absorption

- Eating too fast
- Hairballs
- Intestinal parasites.

(visit www.pets.webmd.com/cat-flatulence-gas for more information)

CHAPTER 14

EDDIE, THE PSYCHOTHERAPUSS

It's a scene anyone who watches talent shows on TV will recognise. A nervous eight-year-old takes to the stage, nervously clutching a microphone, while her family look on from the wings: Mum has tears in her eyes, Dad mouths a few words of encouragement. The audience falls silent and after taking a moment to compose themselves the child starts to sing. Her voice isn't just good, it's incredible: she has the sound, depth and soul of a forty-year-old, even though she's much younger. She sings about a broken heart, and you find yourself believing her, and she leaves you with a feeling that you've just experienced something unique, something truly special, something heaven sent...

So what's all this got to do with Eddie? Well, he was that kid. He didn't sing, yet for me he was a celestial being covered in fur whose noble silence spoke a thousand words.

I had left home early to get to Eddie's groom on time as his owner lived some way across town. All I knew was that he was a large black cat and I expected, due to the short-notice booking, that he would require a thorough 'dematting'. His owner sounded desperate, and, although I have to be choosy about just how far I travel, I never like to let down anyone who sounds as if they're in need.

After a buzz of the doorbell a smiley middle-aged lady greeted me and led me into her living room, where Eddie was waiting on the dining table. It sounds silly, but he reminded me of a wise old friendly barn owl. He was sitting upright, his paws neatly placed before his body – a beautiful cat pose that any lover of felines will recognise. His eyes were wide and warm, and although he didn't move to greet me, I felt welcomed as he observed calmly from a distance.

'Hello bubba,' I said, presenting my hand to him for a sniff.

This is the cat equivalent of a handshake and it's good manners before you start to pet or handle them. I'm in the habit of calling all my cats 'Bubba' or 'Bubbles', which must leave both the animals and their owners mystified, maybe even irritated. Still, when you deal with dozens of cats a week it's a nightmare trying to remember all their names. Unperturbed by his new moniker, Eddie nudged into my hand and started purring. I gave him a catnip mouse to complete the introduction.

'So what exactly needs doing?' I asked, noticing Eddie's fur looked and felt like silk.

'I think he needs a bath,' said Gill, the owner. 'Don't you think his coat looks greasy? I thought he could do with a nice spa day.'

The word 'spa' used in connection with cats always riles me. Often owners see a groom as the feline equivalent of a luxury human pampering session: it is not. For many cats the removal of serious matting is necessary for their general health. In addition, unless a cat is introduced to water baths from a young age, a thorough scrub in the tub followed by clipping is far from relaxing – it can turn into a terrifying ordeal. For this reason I don't usually recommend bathing a cat. Given the stress it puts them under, it is not always worth it. This was one such situation and some tact was required.

'I don't think Eddie could be more magnificent if he tried. He's probably the cleanest cat that's ever been presented to me,' I said, laughing and hoping desperately that Gill would agree. But out of the blue her face crumpled and she started sobbing.

'He's so beautiful,' I said, 'what's the matter?'

Meanwhile Eddie nudged me again, burying his face into my side from his perch on the table as if thanking me for the compliment.

Gill slumped, embarrassed, into the sofa.

'I'm so sorry, I'm having a bit of a bad day. My boss mistakenly copied me into an email, which was unflattering about me and critical of my work. It has left me feeling very upset.'

Now, I don't have a degree in psychology, I only have one in cat behaviour, but I could see what was going on here: Gill, feeling down in the dumps about herself, was projecting those feelings on to Eddie and wanted him to enjoy a treat that might in turn cheer her up too. I momentarily thought of popping her in a bubble bath and later combing her wet hair on the grooming table, and just about managed to stop myself from laughing.

As I handed Gill a tissue, Eddie batted the catnip mouse I had given him in her direction. When it plopped on the floor by her feet she began to giggle. Eddie looked so pleased with himself and stared at her with that serene, knowing face. It was mesmerising.

Gill and I continued chatting, and for a moment I forgot about the groom. Eddie jumped into her lap, purring, and sat gazing into her eyes.

'He does this when I'm upset,' she sobbed. 'I dry my tears on his fur.'

It was remarkable. Eddie seemed to sense his owner's sadness and I don't think it was coincidence that he punched the mouse towards her feet, managing to suddenly lighten the mood. Then he had taken to her lap, offering Gill the comfort of a warm and cuddly companion. There was a definite glint in his eyes when he stared, as if trying to draw her into a carefree catty world.

Gill kindly made some delicious hot chocolate and we chatted on for an hour or so. I gently explained that I wouldn't bath Eddie because it was unnecessary and putting a cat through such stress for no reason is something I wouldn't do. For this reason my equipment remained untouched and I devoted myself to cheering Gill up instead.

'I feel so silly,' she told me as she accompanied me to my car, looking much perkier. 'I wasn't expecting such a reaction.'

'That's okay, it's all in a day's work,' I said, like a cheerful window cleaner on his rounds.

We said goodbye and I gave Gill a big hug.

'You look after yourself and Eddie. He's a very special cat.'

Driving home, I felt very relaxed and I supposed Eddie had worked his magic not only on Gill, but also on me. He's another cat whose memory will stay with me for ever. He really should open up his own practice. I would be first in line for Eddie, the beautiful, talented and intuitive psychotherapuss.

🐾 Mog Tip: Cats and Humans

We cat owners have a very special bond with our pets. What we get from them is hard to explain to anyone who doesn't own a cat or isn't that into animals. We love the fact that cats, like all animals, live in the now. To communicate with another species that sees life so differently from us, and yet manages to adapt to life with us every day, is amazingly inspiring – even more so when a cat with psychological baggage can learn to trust humans again. The ways they show us they are happy to be with us are very endearing, such as the cute head-butts or wrapping around our legs, purring.

We have given them the power to lift the lowest of our spirits. Their large wide almond eyes, disproportionate to the size of their heads, resemble a baby and so bring out our nurturing side. We also love their curious antics – the playful nature of cats sees them in funny, awkward situations, which again make us laugh, endearing them to us even more; hence the thousands of YouTube videos showing cats getting up to all sorts.

Cats are very independent creatures and the most stoic of survivors but they can also be wonderful companions. Caring for any animal brings out a tender side in us all and research shows that stroking an animal can relieve tension and anxieties, so reducing our blood pressure and therefore the chances of heart attacks or strokes: they are the ultimate stress-busters.

Because cats bring out the nurturing side in us, many owners call them 'fur babies', some using them as a child substitute. And yes, my husband and I are among the latter! Animals can teach us patience, love and kindness, but above all, how to live in the moment. In a world where we hardly look up from our phones, the rewards that come from sharing life with a cat are priceless.

CHAPTER 15

LITTLE WOLF – A KITTY HELEN KELLER

Striding past an old shop doorway the passer-by stopped and listened. Sure enough, there was a cat crying. Turning around, the pedestrian looked into the gloomy entrance and there, huddled terrified in the corner, was a black-and-white British Longhair; he had been dumped by his previous owners like a worthless piece of litter.

Although they were hurrying to work, the kindly person knew they couldn't just leave a cat suffering and mercifully scooped up the frightened timid animal into their arms, dropping him off at a local rescue centre. It was here that staff named him 'Little Wolf' and soon discovered this was no ordinary cat: he was deaf and blind and made a huge impact on all who met him.

To help him find his feet the centre initially homed Little Wolf with a fosterer called Jodi and it was she who contacted me to ask if I could help with his smelly matted coat. It would be my first-ever groom of a deaf and blind cat, so I knew when handling him I would have to be extremely sensitive, especially as the little chap would need a potentially traumatic bath.

Yet when I met Little Wolf I was amazed. For a cat who had been treated so badly he was very trusting and despite his disabilities he walked with a surprising air of confidence. Although he couldn't see or hear, he had figured out his way around Jodi's home, managing to climb the stairs and even jump on the bed. He had bonded extremely well with her, following her everywhere and clinging to her side at night. I wasn't surprised to discover he had worked his way into her heart and although she already owned two other cats, she was thinking about adopting him.

I gave Little Wolf the usual catnip mouse as I set

up my grooming table. Jodi prepared a bowl of his favourite tinned tuna for me to feed him, which would also encourage a positive association in his mind. Using Little Wolf's main sense, smell, was hugely important in building his confidence around me so I sprayed synthetically produced cat pheromones on my clothes.

The moment Little Wolf was placed on the table I knew he felt out of his comfort zone. After all, he had no idea of where he was now standing. Jodi and I both stroked his head and face, but he remained nervous as I started grooming. Luckily he couldn't hear my clippers, so in this case his disability actually worked in his favour. However, the feel of the equipment against his coat was alien to him and he wouldn't settle, choosing to cry out and shift constantly in my arms.

The light-bulb moment came when I remembered Jodi saying Little Wolf never left her side and curled up on her lap on the sofa. It was even difficult for her to get up to make a cup of tea because he would cling to her legs as she stood up. I asked Jodi to sit on the sofa and placed Little Wolf on her lap. Bingo! His anxiety seemed to melt away as he sprawled in Jodi's arms and he purred so loudly it lit up the room. With him stretched out and relaxed, I managed to clip all the matts from his body. A tense situation had turned into a dream groom; I could see why Jodi had fallen head over heels for him.

Of course we weren't finished yet. The bath, potentially even more challenging than the clipping, was next. I slowly lowered Little Wolf onto a rubber mat in the bath; half expecting him to struggle free and run for cover. Astoundingly, he sat calmly as I cupped water in my hands and released it over his back. Even though we had just met, he trusted me totally. Next, I lathered up the cat shampoo until he was covered in suds. His disability again worked in my favour when I started up the showerhead. He couldn't hear the flow of water, nor could he see the dirty water that flowed from his body and left the bath a muddy brown colour – it showed just how filthy he had been.

Thankfully the dryer was the one part of the groom that Little Wolf really loved. Feeling the light warm air caressing his skin, he stretched out in total bliss and even nodded off for a moment. Once totally dry, he looked beautiful. His bib, the name we groomers and breeders use for the hair under the chin, was trimmed and what remained of his fur was silky-smooth: he looked stunning.

I wish I could say that was the end of Little Wolf's story and that Jodi adopted him, finally providing him with the loving forever home he deserved but sometimes things are more complicated. A few days after I left Little Wolf looking like a new cat, his photo appeared on the rescue centre's website together with an appeal for new owners. I thought it must be a mistake and so I called Jodi. Sadly, she had developed an allergy to Little Wolf, possibly from his dander (dry dead skin) or saliva. Sadly these allergies can show themselves from different animals within the same species. After breaking out in a rash and constantly sneezing and coughing, Jodi had little choice but to return him. It was devastating for all concerned.

Given Little Wolf's disabilities and needs, it would take some time before a suitable guardian came along. During this time he was depressed and withdrawn – no wonder after feeling such much love and tenderness for a fosterer he probably thought would be with him until the end. Eventually fate smiled on Little Wolf once again and he was rehomed by a lovely couple who fell for the beautiful cat huddled in the back of his cage, seemingly staring into space.

I still groom Little Wolf and I'm delighted he enjoys the love and stability he needs and deserves. He has an enclosed courtyard, where he loves to lie in the sun and nibble on rows of fresh grass, his purpose-built salad bar.

He really is the sweetest, most inspiring kitty Helen Keller in town.

🐾 Mog Tip: Allergic to Cats?

Many cat owners suffer each day with cold-like symptoms (wheezing, coughing, red itchy eyes or a runny nose, or all four symptoms) due to being allergic to their pets. Some people suffer side effects so badly that they cannot stay in the same room as a cat. So, what causes a person to be allergic to cats? The answer is not the fur but tiny proteins in the cat's saliva, urine and dander (dry flakes of skin). Some cats are said to be hypoallergenic (relatively unlikely to cause an allergic reaction), such as the Siberian and Balinese breeds, but even then a cat can still cause a problem with someone who has a weak immune system and suffers allergies. The reason some cats are labelled as hypoallergenic is because they produce fewer allergens than others. Cats do produce pet dander, a common allergen, but the chief culprit for the estimated 10 per cent of the population who are allergic to cats may be a protein, Fel d 1, that is present in cat saliva. Some ways to alleviate symptoms are over-the-counter medications such as antihistamines, daily hoovering of pet hair from furnishings, pet bedding, carpets and restricted areas such as the bed, where dander will accumulate. Products like Petal Cleanse shampoo can also help.

Many groomers believe that bathing a cat will reduce dander but Dr Robert Zuckerman, an allergy and asthma specialist in Philadelphia, USA (who I regularly follow for current advice), feels differently. Writing on the consciouscat website, he says: 'Bathing a cat was once believed to be helpful but the cat would have to be washed almost daily. Instead, daily use of products such as Pal's Quick Cleansing Wipes™ will remove saliva and dander from your cat's hair and are less stressful for felines who prefer not to be rubbed in the tub.' That is very good advice and I totally agree. Also, try to keep healthy with daily vitamins and minerals to help support your immune system.

Here are a couple of interesting websites where you can find more information:

- www.petmd.com/cat/wellness/evr_ct_hypoallergenic_cat_breeds
- www.consciouscat.net/2011/08/29/living-with-cat-allergies-and-cats/

CHAPTER 16

LUCKY, THE MIRACLE TUBE CAT

The annoying beep of a text roused me from my slumbers at 7.59am, calling a halt to a lovely dream involving the rather attractive Cillian Murphy. I'd been watching him as bad boy Tommy Shelby in the excellent BBC series *Peaky Blinders* the night before.

I always think someone contacting me particularly early or late must be the bearer of bad news, so I reached for my mobile, squinting anxiously and bleary-eyed at the screen.

CLAWS

Hi Anita, I am Lucy, the owner of the cat Lucky, who was stuck in a Tube tunnel on the London Underground for 3 days. I don't know if you've seen it on the news? Lucky is in a bad way and is tremendously dirty after her ordeal. She is white and tabby normally, but desperate for a clean. I tried to bathe her yesterday but it was difficult and I need some help. Please can you get back to me? I'm hoping you have some space today for a home visit. I'm based in Clapham. Thanks for your reply. Best, Lucy.

I hadn't seen the news, but I certainly wanted to know more about the cat who had gone exploring in the Underground and miraculously lived to tell the tale.

It didn't take long to find the story online. After all, it was featured on the websites of some of the biggest newspapers in the country, including the *Mirror*, *The Sun*, *The Daily Telegraph* and the *Evening Standard*. It was easy to see why Lucky's survival against the odds had struck a chord with so many people. Lucy and Lucky had been on a trip to Somerset and were travelling back on the Victoria Line during a busy weekend when Lucky somehow escaped from her carrier at Green Park station.

Lucy watched helpless as the terrified puss darted through people's legs before diving from the platform to the Underground tracks below. Her attempts to call back her beloved pet proved futile, and the last she saw of Lucky was her little white legs vanishing into the tunnel, heading in the direction of Oxford Circus. Naturally Lucy waited to see if Lucky would return, but after several hours she headed home, mentally and physically exhausted.

Before turning in for the night, Lucy decided to share the tragic tale online and also began a campaign to find Lucky. When she woke up the next morning, many of her friends had tweeted the hashtag #findLucky and it wasn't long before the tale went viral. Sympathetic London Underground staff got on board to help, and on this rare occasion, even allowed Lucy onto the tracks to call for her cat after the Tube had closed. Her shouts echoed eerily along the tunnels, but sadly there were no meows or chirps in response.

Three days passed and Lucy had virtually given up

hope when she received the call she thought would never come. A Transport for London worker had spotted Lucky at Oxford Circus station, looking slightly worse for wear but hungrily chewing on a mouse. The RSPCA were called and Lucky was eventually captured. While the animal charity wanted to sedate Lucky to clean her up, Lucy, understandably, just wanted her fur baby home: she had been put through enough. Once Lucky was settled, Lucy texted me to see if I could help by giving her a good bath. I was only too happy to help.

Lucy wasn't home from work when my husband Gordon and I arrived at her pretty garden flat. Her partner, Alex, welcomed us inside, apparently somewhat unfazed by the ordeal that had befallen the feline.

'Lucky doesn't like men,' he explained matter-of-factly, shaking Gordon's hand before taking us to Lucky in the living room. She lay curled in her favourite bed, a tiny, timid-looking creature covered head to toe in oil and layer upon layer of dirt. When I sat quietly beside her and ran my hand gently over her back my fingers came away black with grime.

At first Lucky didn't move, still no doubt recovering

from her trauma. However, eventually she began nudging my hand and purring appreciatively. It was hard to imagine her spending three terrifying days in the alien environment of the Underground with trains hurtling over her tiny frame as she cowered for safety.

When Lucy arrived it was lovely to finally meet the determined and devoted woman I'd read about in so many newspapers. I could tell she had a deep connection with Lucky.

'I think it's a miracle my baby is home,' she said, looking over at the bundle of oily, matted fur. 'Thank you so much for coming over at such short notice.'

For a brief instant I thought of Cillian wearing nothing but his flat cap, and then pinched myself.

'No problem at all.'

The bathing process had to be as stress-free as possible, which was a tall order given that Lucky had never experienced a professional groom, never mind one involving water and shampoo. I set the men to work clearing the area around the kitchen sink and filling saucepans and jugs with warm water. A large bath towel was placed in the sink to give Lucky something soft and non-slippery to stand on. The warm water would be slowly introduced to her body to see how she responded.

With everything in place I donned my waterproof paw-print apron and with some help from Lucy, deposited Lucky carefully into the sink. For a cat that had been through so much, Lucky's reaction to the water was surprisingly gentle. She didn't enjoy the process, but not once did she try to scratch or bite me – unlike some of my other furry clients. Ahem!

I frequently care for cats who seem to understand I'm there to help, and Lucky's brave behaviour suggested she was one such puss. Of course having her mummy by her side must have been reassuring, for Lucy rained endless kisses down on her little one's head.

After dampening Lucky's grimy fur, I reached for the bottle of powerful degreasing pet shampoo I'd ordered from the USA. Finally it would come in useful and I would get to try it on a truly dirty cat. I lathered Lucky up until she looked like a mini yeti who'd called to the parlour for a shampoo and set.

Every so often I called out, 'More water!' It was like

a typical scene from a cowboy film. You know the one – as flames grip a wooden family home, the caring townsfolk line up to pass buckets of water down the line to douse the fire and save the day.

Once the suds were gone from Lucky's coat, a quick shower was necessary to remove any shampoo that had been massaged deep into her fur. Thankfully Lucky responded well to being transported from the kitchen sink to the bathtub, where she was lightly hosed down. After a couple of one-minute showers, with a break for reassuring cuddles in between, her fur was finally oil- and shampoo-free. I finished the groom off with my hairdryer on a low setting. The blow-dry left Lucky looking fantastic – that oil-slicked fur was now gleaming and soft as silk.

Some cats like to hide after a groom, but sweet Lucky sat a foot away, giving herself a once-over with her tongue. This is a normal feline response to being shampooed as the fur is covered in a strange scent. Later, Lucky even allowed me to stroke her again, and she posed perfectly for several photographs. It was as if she was beginning to get used to the limelight.

Lucky's rescue was a team effort. From the pet-loving public's tweets and shared posts on social media through to London Underground staff, TFL workers and the RSPCA and, finally, yours truly, the groomer. Afterwards I felt inspired and warm inside, honoured to have played a small part in such a feel-good story.

Lucky by name and extremely lucky by nature.

Mog Tip: Does Your Cat Need a Bath?

Most cats do not need regular bathing and can cope perfectly well when it comes to keeping themselves clean but with mogs that desperately need our help in extreme circumstances, such as Lucky, the key is speed and gentle handling. A cat may find water very stressful and will panic, not understanding what is going on. It is advisable to ask a professional holistic cat groomer to assist in bathing your cat, should they need a good clean from oil, dirt or other stubborn debris. Bathing in the incorrect way can lead to scratches and bites as your cat fights tooth and nail to escape the spray of the shower. For slight accidents in the nether regions a warm wet cloth or commercial cat body wipes can be a cheaper alternative. Always ensure the product is specifically designed to be used on cats as some ingredients, if designed to be used on

humans or other animals, may be harmful to cats.
I personally like the John Paul brand of pet wipes.

CHAPTER 17

LITTLE MISS SLEEPYHEAD

The door swung open to reveal an instantly recognisable male celebrity beaming his trademark winning smile.

My heart skipped a beat, but I reined in my emotions and drew a poker face.

'Hi there, cat groomer here!' I said brightly, realising that a bag bulging with brushes, combs and clippers had almost certainly already given the game away.

'Ah yes,' said the man I will call 'Mr D'. 'Come in. Would you like a coffee?'

I declined the kind invitation of an ice-breaking beverage and entered his large beautifully decorated home only for my nerves to suddenly get the better of me. I heard myself rambling on about traffic, parking, how I like to arrive for bookings early – basically anything to stop blurting out, 'Oh gosh, you're that bloke off the telly – can we have a selfie together?'

A stunning black-and-grey blind cat casually entered the scene, mercifully calling a halt to my attack of verbal diarrhoea. Teabag was a rescue cat from north-west Italy. Her mother delivered the litter right in the street of Liguria, Manarola, part of the Cinque Terre National Park, and little Teabag popped out, blind as a bat.

Mr and Mrs D were regular visitors to Liguria and realised the plight of the blind little kitty that was being fed by villagers but clearly faced a huge challenge if she was to survive on the streets. With their heartstrings well and truly tugged, and following advice from various animal charities, as well as the UK Home Office, the couple started the complicated process of adopting not only Teabag, but also her brother Frodo. The bureaucracy was staggering and they had to take care of pet passports, inoculations, microchipping, rabies injections, a vet's certificate, transport and further necessary paperwork.

It was all worth it when several weeks later, Teabag and Frodo arrived at their new home, over 800 miles away in London. The Italian kitty had clearly settled in to her luxury surroundings and began smelling her way through the equipment in my bag, venturing to the legs of the grooming table and finishing up with me. Blind cats have to be approached in a different way to their seeing counterparts, so I sat on the floor and allowed her plenty of time to become accustomed to my smell and voice.

'She's a wonderful cat,' said Mr D, scooping up Teabag affectionately and handing her to me like a baby, tummy side up. I always get uncomfortable seeing cats being held that way, with their sensitive underside exposed to the world. No wonder Teabag looked so apprehensive. After all, there was a stranger in her home with unusual equipment that smelt of other cats, and suddenly Daddy was passing her round in her most vulnerable position. I wasn't surprised when, five minutes into the groom,

Miss T began to show signs of stress. Her matted belly needed shaving, but each time I tried to get close with the clippers her eyes widened.

'Teabag is okay, isn't she?' Mr D asked repeatedly, despite my assurances she was fine.

After a few unsuccessful attempts with the clippers I finally accepted the offer of coffee to give Teabag and the rest of us a break, while Mr D and I chatted over a cuppa.

'So what happens now?' asked Mr D, looking down at the ball of fluff excitedly bunny-kicking her new toy.

'There's still a lot of fur to come off,' I replied. 'Let's try again to see how she fares.'

'She will be alright, won't she?' he asked yet again.

'Yes, of course,' I said, looking at Teabag enjoying herself on the floor of her mansion and immediately hoping I was right to be so optimistic.

I tried grooming Teabag on the floor, on her favourite armchair, in Mr D's arms and on the table. We also tried appeasing her with treats, catnip, face massages and even blowing warm air on her head. I kid you not – most cats love it when owners gently press their lips on the top of their head and slowly blow out a gentle flow of warm breath. Mr D was much amused by the idea and duly pressed his face towards Teabag, but to no effect.

Teabag's increasing jitters and flexing claws were now making shaving treacherous, so I decided it would be kinder to de-matt her under sedation a few days later. I knew what was coming when I explained the plan.

'She will be –'

'Yes,' I interrupted before the sentence was finished. 'She will.'

When Mr D arrived at the veterinary practice the head nurse couldn't believe it. I chuckled to myself as a flirty grin spread over her face from ear to ear. Judging by his smiles I could swear even the vet himself had developed a man-crush on my celebrity client.

Once Teabag was sedated the remainder of the groom didn't take long at all. Her belly was fully shaved, her bib (the thick fur under her chin) thinned, her coat thoroughly combed and finally her nails were clipped before she was ready for the sedation to be reversed.

I like to stay with sedated cats to see them wake up

and gently reassure them that everything is okay. While I was waiting for Teabag to open her eyes hunky Mr D came bounding down the stairs, to the surgery area where I normally groom my sedation cats, like James Bond in pursuit of his latest squeeze. His appearance surprised me because access to the basement is usually restricted, but given that Teabag had a disability, I felt it was probably a good thing for her to awake to a familiar voice. However, awaken she did not – at least not as quickly as expected. Ten minutes, fifteen, twenty, then twenty-five minutes passed and still Little Miss Sleepyhead was not rousing from her beauty sleep.

Under light sedation most cats come round after ten minutes, giving a little grumble or meow. With Teabag's owner waiting desperately to say hello, her silence was uncomfortably deafening.

'Come on, sweetie,' I said, gently moving her into various positions to try and encourage her to wake up. At this Teabag let out a tiny groan like a child reluctant to awake from a dream.

Next, I got a tiny sandbag, used to prop animals up during operations, to place under her head. Now even more comfortable, Teabag seemed to drift off into an even deeper sleep.

'Maybe you should tell her a story,' I suggested to Mr D. 'I've heard you're supposed to do that for people in comas.'

The words had barely left my mouth when I regretted it.

'Don't worry, your cat's not in a coma,' I added before he could ask, 'She will be alright, won't she?' for the umpteenth time.

In the end I called Andrew, the vet. He listened to Teabag's heart and checked her little gums to keep an eye on her circulation: if the gums are a nice pink colour then circulation is good, while a purple tinge indicates circulation is poor. Thankfully Teabag's gums were pink and healthy.

The vet also checked the capillary refill time (CRT) by pressing Teabag's gums until they turned white and timing to see how long it took for them to return to pink. The colour was back in less than two seconds – another sign of good circulation. Everything was as it should be.

'Some cats do take longer,' Andrew said with a relaxed air of authority. 'Nothing to worry about.'

After thirty minutes he decided perhaps a little booster of reverse sedation was necessary, and indeed that did the trick. Soon Teabag was swishing her tail and slowly opening her eyes. Seeing her sit up and get a big kiss from her daddy was a huge relief and easily the best thing that happened to me all day.

Sedation is perfectly safe, but I always hope the moment between the drug being reversed and the cat opening its eyes is quick. I hate the waiting game between consciousness and unconsciousness, when time stands still and I long for the reassuring flicker of an eyelid or a tiny meow.

A few days later, I emailed Mr D to ask how Little Miss Sleepyhead was doing. Ironically I found myself asking, 'She is okay, isn't she?'

Yes, of course she is!

Mog Tip: Rescuing Cats from Abroad

We are a nation of animal lovers and, if you're reading this book, you're no doubt a huge cat lover who may have, on more than one occasion, seen a stray cat or kitten abroad that pulled at your heartstrings. My husband always has to check my suitcase whenever I visit Greece or Turkey due to the amount of cats I fall in love with. I remembered reading an article by Natalie Paris for *The Daily Telegraph* in which she covers this topic very well and in great depth. Some pointers are:

• Cats need to be microchipped (you must make sure the animal has the microchip before the rabies vaccination, otherwise the jab won't count) and receive inoculations. You must also obtain a pet passport and have them treated for flea and ear mites as well as a rabies vaccination followed by a twenty-one-day wait before entering the UK, according to the Home Office. This replaces the need to be quarantined.

• It is also a requirement to travel with an authorised transport company on an authorised route. The costs can mount up but one look from those little almond eyes followed by a squeaky 'take me home' meow will help us forget the instant drainage of our bank accounts and concentrate more on the lifetime of joy and happiness our rescue cat can give us.

Visit the Home Office page for further advice, where it deals with taking pets abroad and bringing them home: www.gov.uk/take-pet-abroad

CHAPTER 18

FISTICUFFS FRANK AND HIS GAME OF 'REVERSE KICK THE CAT'

Towering wrought-iron gates loomed overhead, so I pulled up and texted my client to buzz me into what I assumed was a gated residential complex in leafy Wimbledon, one of my favourite parts of London. I felt a twinge of jealousy when the gates slowly opened to reveal a winding driveway with trees and flowers on either side, and what seemed to be a vast communal garden.

As I parked my car, Hilary descended the steps of the main house and greeted me with a warm, firm handshake. Her smart tweed suit gave her an air of officialdom and confidence, although her manner was far more relaxed.

'What a lovely place you all share,' I blurted out, glancing from the gardens to Hilary's sprawling home to the smaller houses nearby.

'It's not shared,' she laughed. 'Only we live here. Those other buildings are outhouses, a stable and garages.'

'Wow, you've got a beautiful place then!' I smiled, making a mental note to tell her I'd happily house sit the properties and cat sit her moggy any time she liked.

'I'm afraid Frank's gone walkies,' she announced somewhat sheepishly, just before I had a chance to ask the whereabouts of the cat I was there to groom.

That old chestnut, I thought to myself, my heart sinking a little. I hear this on a regular basis from clients with cunning cats who manipulate them into a five-minute jaunt outside just before my arrival. Of course, that five minutes turns out to be anything but.

'Don't worry, he never travels far,' said Hilary, slightly flustered to see my mild frustration. 'He's usually here by the back door.'

I looked around again and shrugged. Clearly this time he wasn't.

Leaving Hilary to look for Frank, I started to unload my equipment. She began at the back door, then moved to the front, then tried calling under the bushes, by the garages and stables and then finally asked the cleaners if they had spotted the errant puss: they hadn't.

'He's never been gone this long,' she spluttered as twenty minutes passed. 'Would you like a coffee perhaps?' she added, showing me indoors and trying to distract me from the elephant in the room – namely that there was still no Frank.

I accepted the offer, thinking of the checklist I send to clients before my visits. Point one is to lock the cat flap the night before, especially for bookings first thing in the morning – just like this one. I really should start to charge for my waiting time!

With mug in hand I did my best to assist as Hilary continued to search for the elusive Frank. I could feel her desperation as she looked under the sofa and had to try not to smile. There was barely room for a mouse to squeeze under it, let alone a cat.

'Do you think Frank is somewhere else in your home? Maybe the cleaners locked him in a room by mistake,' I suggested, trying to be helpful.

'Good point,' said Hilary, before closing the back door and setting off to trawl through the property.

I sipped my coffee and listened to frantic footsteps and doors opening and closing on the various floors above, her calls to Frank becoming fainter and fainter. Then something caught my eye through the cat flap: a black-and-white ball of fluff was staring at me.

'Erm, Hilary,' I shouted, 'Frank's here!'

She quickly abandoned the upper floors and came bounding down the stairs to catch the little tyke before he went missing again.

Frank was fourteen years old, but looked far younger. He was a feisty little fellow and after Hilary's emails about his antics, I was expecting a bumpy ride. Not only did he hate being picked up, he also didn't care much for being groomed either. This meant the fur on his body, which wasn't in the least bit frail as you might expect with an elderly cat, was severely matted.

'Oh, Frank likes his food,' said Hilary somewhat

defensively as I raised an eyebrow at his portly physique. In truth, I like food-orientated cats as they are usually so easy to bribe with treats compared to their fussier counterparts. Severely overweight pets suffer because of their size and are a different matter altogether.

A tin of tuna was duly opened and plonked in front of Frank's twitching nose to keep him occupied while I checked where he most needed shaving: almost everywhere, it seemed.

With my clippers in hand, I got started. Right from the start Frank decided he wasn't going to play ball and no amount of tuna would convince him otherwise. Not only did he yowl and call, every time I touched him or shaved a matt, he lashed out at poor Hilary.

It was a case of 'Reverse Kick the Cat Syndrome', with Frank taking his role as kicker very seriously indeed. The term comes from the tradition of a person in high rank unfairly taking out their frustrations on someone lower down the pecking order. According to author John Bradshaw in his excellent book *Cat Sense*, the phrase originates from the nineteenth century when people thought nothing of kicking cats, or any animal for that matter. Luckily times have changed and while the phrase remains in common parlance, I'm sure few cats are ever actually kicked by someone who is having one of those days.

Frank's paws and razor-sharp nails flashed and flailed as he growled and swatted Hilary throughout the groom. Fortunately she was wearing a thick pair of my protective gloves – RSPCA-endorsed wildlife handling gloves, to be precise. I hadn't had them for long, and Frank put them through their paces. Clearly he was angry at Hilary for agreeing to allow the groom to go ahead. Who knows what thoughts were going through the mog's mind as he glared at his traitorous owner…

'It's all YOUR fault, YOU hired her. YOU let her in our home. YOU sold me out…'

Once I'd finished Frank's lion cut, he was placed on the floor in front of his untouched tuna. He snorted and walked off in a huff towards the living-room window, where he made himself comfortable and glared back at Hilary. Realising there was considerable tension to be diffused I threw Frank a catnip mouse and began packing up. As I was leaving, I looked over my shoulder just in time to see Frank spaced out, drooling over the now-soggy toy.

Ah ha, got ya! I thought, making my way to the car. No cat has ever been able to resist my emergency Catnip Zebedee mice, stuffed with a natural herb from the mint family called *Nepeta cataria*, which gives felines a harmless fifteen-minute high.

As I pulled away from the beautiful house Hilary was waving me off, apparently oblivious to her fur-covered tweed. As I wound down my window, on the verge of offering my services as a house sitter, I could see myself swanning like the lady of the manor from room to room, sipping fresh lemonade on the manicured lawn while Frank lazed nearby. Then I remembered the little terror's outstretched paws and claws and thought better of it. I returned Hilary's friendly wave and wound the window up again while negotiating the twisting drive. After all, there was no telling what would happen if this four-legged lord of the manor played 'Reverse Kick the Cat' with me!

🐾 Mog Tip: Do You Have a Cat That Loves to Kick?

I have found the perfect toys for our bunny-kicking felines: the Kong Cat Kickaroo™. These soft toys are oblong and the perfect shape for a cat to wrap its arms and back legs around to give a good old kicking. Some are infused with catnip to drive your cat even wilder and keep them well away from targeting our hands and other body parts! They're available from most pet product outlets.

CHAPTER 19

FOUR CRANKY CATS AND A BRUSH WITH THE OLD BILL

The door to the basement flat stood ever so slightly ajar, so I pushed it open and announced my arrival.

'Hi there, it's Anita here. Shall I come on in?'

No answer. Unsure whether to proceed, I slowly picked my way along a short corridor to the living room, where an elderly man was sitting comfortably in his armchair.

'Oh, hello, I'm sorry to barge in,' I said, feeling a little embarrassed. 'The door was open so I thought it would be okay.'

But the man remained silent and stared straight ahead. To break the ice I reached out to shake his hand and explained I was there about his cats. He returned the handshake but maintained the same poker face.

'Shall I take off my boots?' I asked, realising he was wearing socks and I'd just tramped in from outside.

'Yes,' he replied in a voice that sounded a little hesitant and confused.

'Sorry I'm early,' I rambled on to fill the awkward silence. 'You know how it is in London, you never know how long it will take to get somewhere.'

I was struggling with my laces when I heard someone else approach and turned to see a young man in his twenties or thirties.

'Hi there, I was just apologising to your dad for being early. I'm taking off my boots and then we can get started.'

The newcomer fixed me with a baffled stare.

'Okay, em, who are you exactly?'

The penny dropped. There were none of the usual signs of a cat-filled household. No wisps of hair on the carpet, no clawed furniture, not even a faint smell of cat pee, which thankfully isn't that usual anyway. I'd come to the wrong house.

Thankfully my hosts, one of whom I suspect had Alzheimer's, saw the funny side and I was directed to a dingy nearby flat where the desperate resident had booked me, as a qualified feline behaviourist, to help with his troubled cats.

My behavioural consultations are vet referrals, and in an initial email from the client he explained that one of the cats, Oliver, was attacking the other three. We emailed back and forth a few times to confirm the fee and appointment, and then the client revealed that as he would be travelling for work I would actually be dealing with his three twenty-something brothers on the day. As he was the main pet guardian it wasn't ideal, but I do try to be flexible and provide a convenient service that works around people's busy lives.

As soon as I entered the flat I sensed tension in the air: it was suffocating. No sooner had I asked the three siblings to describe the problem than they all began to confide in me about their hatred of living with so many troublesome cats. At this point a dog – a Collie/

Staffie cross – ambled nonchalantly out of one room and disappeared into another. I asked if there were any other residents I didn't yet know about. Luckily there weren't, so this meant the tiny flat was being shared by four grown men, four fretting felines and one seriously outnumbered pooch.

I was trying to be sympathetic as the barrage of complaints continued, when a domestic short-haired cat came striding into the room. It had to be Oliver, a former stray who had been adopted by his well-meaning owner. He trotted over and seemed friendly at first, giving my hand a gentle sniff. Then, just when I thought we had made friends, he administered a cheeky nip and wandered off as if nothing was amiss.

Thanks a lot, I thought.

Next, the brothers introduced me to the three other cats, who were nervously hunkering down in various cubbyholes and hiding places to keep away from vicious Oliver. When I saw the terror on their little faces I realised just what a dire situation I had been asked to address. Here were three highly-strung brothers who resented sharing their home with their elusive brother's pets. They told me he was away quite a lot, so I felt sure the animals were picking up on the stressful atmosphere they endured when their owner was gone.

It would be extremely difficult for me to change this situation. For a start, cats don't do well indoors in close proximity to one another when the territory is small. Many environmental changes would be required to bring peace to this fractious multi-cat household, but who could I rely upon to see them implemented?

Tensions were rising as we talked through the various options. Every question I asked was met with voices getting louder and louder: the brothers weren't just taking their frustration out on each other, they were starting to turn on me too. Thankfully my phone rang and things calmed slightly while I spoke to Derek, the client, who was calling from overseas to hear my feedback. I would have to be honest and say this wouldn't be easy.

'We are in a terrible situation,' I told him. 'Three terrified cats are hiding and your brothers aren't happy. For this to work, I need you to be here.'

I took a deep breath, because I knew what I had to say next would come as a shock.

'Bearing the cramped conditions in mind, I think you should re-home Oliver. I could help you find a nice home for him, preferably with a garden. You mentioned he was once a stray so he's used to being outdoors and his frustration at being inside may well be contributing to his aggression.'

This was met with a harsh rebuff.

'Absolutely not,' said Derek. 'I could never give up on him, that is not going to happen.'

I pleaded with him to see the situation in a different way. It wasn't a case of giving up on Oliver, but rather offering a more suitable home that would provide him, and consequently his three kitty colleagues, with a better life. It's a bitter pill to swallow, but often the best thing a loving owner can do is put their pet's well-being above their own feelings.

After continuing along this path for a while I realised I was talking to a brick wall. Derek had ceased listening. He asked to speak to one of his brothers, so I handed over the phone, feeling altogether deflated.

When Derek eventually rang off you could have cut the atmosphere with a knife. The brothers, having heard me fail to convince him of the right thing to do, began to turn on each other in frustration. Accusations flew about everything from misbehaving moggies to unwashed dishes. All decorum went out the window and the shouting grew louder and louder.

Conscious these were family matters and that I was there to sort the cats, I removed myself from the fracas to check on one of the pets I'd seen hiding in the back bedroom wardrobe. I was halfway down the narrow corridor when all hell broke loose. There was a huge bang and I turned to see chairs and fists flying as two of the brothers started to knock the stuffing out of each other. I instinctively went into Batwoman mode and rushed towards the most aggressive of the culprits, grabbing him tightly by the waist and hauling him away from his victim. There was no time to think of my safety, although reflecting back I grimace at the thought I could have been seriously hurt. In the aftermath the four cats were scurrying around terrified and looking for somewhere to hide. Even the nonchalant dog was howling. It was surreal, horrible and left me feeling physically sick. I was concerned for the animals, but also for the family. There were a lot of issues simmering beneath the surface – issues well beyond the scope of my degree in feline behaviour.

When the brawling men were safely separated into different rooms, someone called the police. Apparently this wasn't the first time they'd clashed. Initially I decided to stay, not only to keep the feuding family members apart, but to make sure no harm came to their pets until the situation had well and truly calmed down.

When the first copper walked in he looked me up and down.

'Are you Mrs…?'

He thought I was the matriarch of the family.

'Erm, no,' I smiled. 'I'm the cat behaviourist.'

'Yeah, whatever,' he replied with an air of sarcasm.

By now my nerves were already shattered so, after that curt response, I decided maybe I wouldn't wait around after all.

'Well, if I'm not needed, I'll be off then,' I said, gathering my bag.

'Hang on, we need your details as a witness to the events,' the policeman said, quickly producing a pen and notepad. I duly gave him my address and phone number before bidding goodbye to the brothers and promising to be in touch.

On the way to the car I reflected on what I'd just experienced. It was no wonder the cats were all at war: just as the family was falling apart, so too were their pets. It's no old wives' tale that cats pick up on the energies of the humans with whom they share their habitat, and this has a huge impact on their behaviour.

Just as I was about to drive off I realised I'd dropped my notebook in the midst of the chaos. I could have kicked myself because now I would have to go back. The book was full of important case notes connected to my visit as well as details on the behaviour of cats that I had groomed. Much as I wanted to, I couldn't just leave it behind.

When I returned to the scene three additional officers had arrived in a van, demonstrating just how seriously the Met were taking the incident. I introduced myself again and explained I'd left my notebook behind.

'And what's your relationship to the family?' asked one of the officers, raising an eyebrow.

I cringed as I replied, 'I'm the cat behaviourist.'
The looks from the three of them said it all.
'Yeah, whatever.'

🐾 Mog Tip: When to Re-home

Most owners love their pets and will move mountains to ensure they get the best life possible. However, sometimes the need to keep our cats living with us can lead to poor judgement and wrong decisions based on what *we* want, rather than the overall well-being of the cat. I know the decision to re-home a cat in situations such as stressful multi-cat households is the last thing an owner wishes to make: they tell me they feel they are letting their cat down. In fact, I feel they are doing the exact opposite. When an owner clearly sees the anxiety some cats live with daily, yet decides to find a home more suitable for their cat in the current situation, it is the kindest and most loving action one can take and shows that the owner is putting the needs of their pet first. It shows great love and bravery to let go and do what is right.

When it comes to behavioural cases, I do everything I can to make situations better for all concerned, but I also have to tell owners when I feel it is time to make other arrangements for the best outcome for the cats involved. The key to dealing with feline behavioural issues is to take action quickly. Find a good accredited cat behaviourist who can visit the home and offer advice, support and a solid plan for moving forward. A behaviourist wants the best outcome for the owners and the cats, but also understands the heartache involved when tough decisions have to be made.

For more information on my cat behavioural home visits, please see www.catbehaviourist.com

CHAPTER 20

BOYD, 'THE OLD TART'

When visiting clients nothing makes me more anxious than the dread of not being able to find a parking space. Often I end up having to drive around for ages in search of a bay suitable for non-residents. Sometimes roads are so narrow and the traffic so heavy that even just pulling over to unload my gear is enough to cause a huge jam.

And so it was that, on a cold winter's night, I drove into a tight London street at the height of rush hour, unwittingly followed by several drivers taking a shortcut. Cars already lined either side, leaving very little room for the two-way traffic to pass. Sweat was dripping down my back as I wondered how I was going to park and unload my table amid the endless revving vehicles being driven by people who just wanted to get home from work. Spotting a house with an empty drive, I quickly pulled into the space, praying the owners wouldn't arrive back any time soon, and rushed to my client Debbie's house almost directly opposite to ask if there might be somewhere to park nearby.

I had only just knocked on the door when a car moved from a space right outside my client's home and as soon as Debbie appeared, she realised the opportunity.

'Quick, you need to nab that space while you can! I'll stop anyone trying to take it.'

Debbie bravely stood in the middle of the spot, defiantly waving on those who tried to pull in. Unfortunately, an endless flow of traffic was stopping me from getting out of the drive on the other side of the street. When a break eventually occurred I reversed at such an awkward angle that it was impossible to straighten up and negotiate my way into the parking space Debbie was guarding so efficiently.

I wound down my window, hot and panicked.

'Parking isn't my best trait,' I confessed apologetically, as more vehicles entered the road from either end. Luckily Debbie was sympathetic.

'Don't worry,' she soothed, 'everything's going to be okay. We'll get you in.'

For several minutes I went backwards and forwards with my client calling out instructions as well as her catchphrase: 'That's it, a bit to the right, now straighten up. Everything's going to be okay!'

At one point I thought an impatient driver was about to get out of his car and do the parking for me, but then after twenty to thirty manoeuvres I made it. I've never been more relieved... Or sweaty.

After a round of handshakes Debbie and her husband Philip brought me inside to meet Boyd, a cute ginger stray. He seemed relaxed, but I knew not to be lulled into a false sense of security. Boyd had built up quite a reputation thanks to a visit to the vet, during which he scuppered an attempt to trim his nails. Quite an achievement for a tiny mog! His owners told me that he hated being held or stroked unless it was on his terms. In fact Debbie's warning from the initial phone consultation was ringing in my ears: 'Boyd doesn't like being handled. He complains verbally, then physically. First with paws, then with claws.'

I got the message.

As I set up the grooming table, Boyd sniffed the air, taking in all the new smells I had carried in from the world outside. Then Philip cracked open his favourite Dreamies treats.

'Come on, you old tart…'

I'd never heard anyone call a cat a tart before, let alone an old one, and on the spur of the moment I couldn't resist a harmless quip.

'Who me?' I said, with a slight chuckle.

Philip didn't laugh, so I cleared my throat and finished setting up.

As soon as Boyd was placed on the table he was firing out hot breath like an enraged dragon, the threatening hisses followed by screeches, with claws and teeth being brandished as though this was a fight to the death. He was acting rather silly – after all, the groom itself hadn't even commenced yet.

I switched on my iPod, hoping some special relaxing cat music might help. Tunes for our feline friends are actually very popular these days. Musician David Teie's *Music for Cats* album (see also page 86) has been a huge success for Universal. He previously played for Metallica, although you'd never guess it from the gentle strains on the soundtrack.

Alas the tinkling music had no impact on boisterous Boyd, whose caterwauling made it barely audible. It wasn't a case of him being afraid; he was angry, affronted, well and truly outraged. Boyd was used to getting his own way and before I arrived even a little growl would normally send his owners packing.

Well, Boyd my boy, I thought, *Times have changed.*

It was rather ironic that Boyd only required some matting on his back to be shaved out. From his petulant antics you'd have thought I was there to cut off his nethers, legs, paws – and eventually his head too. I set to work with my gloves for protection, stopping once in a while for Boyd to nibble on a Dreamie or one of those 'meat lollies', my term for the meaty sticks that cats devour in a flash. I began to realise that in Boyd's mind his behaviour was being rewarded with scrummy treats, so his antics only worsened. He did his best to chew my fingers, but he was no match for my thick gloves, which go up past the elbow; the little bunny kicks didn't get me either.

Watching all this from the sidelines, Philip laughed on numerous occasions and made the odd attempt to calm his charge with praise and sweet talk. There were even a few utterances of 'Boyd, you old tart!'

During a break, Philip went to grab a post-work drink while Debbie and I chatted about Boyd. I could see the house had a large back garden, yet poor Boyd was being kept as an indoor cat. This was odd for a young feline with bags of curiosity and energy to burn off. I appreciated there was a busy road outside, but the back of the house could be professionally cat-proofed, giving him a safe place to play. I'd soon won Debbie over to my way of thinking and when Philip returned he was met by a very enthusiastic pair of ladies discussing what Boyd would get up to in his secure outdoor space.

'Oh no he won't,' said Philip, his face like thunder as he stared at his wife.

I should have kept my mouth shut, but before I knew what I was doing something slipped out.

'It's two against one.'

But Philip ignored me.

'Boyd does fine indoors,' he said, attempting to put a firm stop to the conversation.

'It's your choice, but I think it would be good for him,' I said gently, hoping this wasn't overstepping the mark.

Throughout this standoff Boyd was busily munching away at his treats, his furry cheeks full of food. Philip scooped him up and repositioned him on the table for the remainder of the groom to be completed. The hissy fit recommenced until the last of the remaining matts were gone, and the session was finished with a very quick comb-through. I also gave Debbie and Philip some advice on how to familiarise their beloved Boyd with being touched and groomed so he wouldn't act up in future.

On the way out I had to step over my feline adversary,

who was now stretched on the floor by the front door. I had to admire his fighting spirit. When Philip was distracted, I quickly whispered to Debbie: 'I'll send you a link to some cat-proofing companies. You'll be surprised how good they are.'

She gave me a conspiratorial wink and wished me a safe journey home. Philip hadn't heard a thing. No wonder my husband says that when I get an idea I'm like a 'bulldog with a bit between its teeth'.

Thankfully the traffic had cleared by the time I left, and on the way home I thought more about Boyd's predicament and became even more determined to champion his rights to the back garden – even if he had been less than a perfect little gentleman. Who knows, maybe access to the great outdoors would calm his feistiness too.

The next morning I got up early to email Debbie, as promised. I covered the benefits of providing outside space, not just for the cat but for the owners too. For example, in summertime the patio doors and windows could be opened without the need to constantly battle Boyd's inevitable and understandable attempts to escape. If they really wanted to spoil him they could provide an outdoor water fountain, which many cats prefer to a plain old bowl of water. At the bottom I included links to several cat-proofing companies, as well as some suggestions for suitable combs and toys. I wished them well and asked them to keep me posted.

If I got my way, it was going to be an early Christmas for one old tart – and thankfully I usually do.

🐾 Mog Tip: Do Cats Need Outside Space?

This area has proved to be somewhat controversial, with bird and wildlife lovers insisting cats should be kept permanently inside due to the falling wildlife population, and the polar opposite side stating that all cats should be free-roaming. Even entire countries have different opinions on the issue. In most of the USA, the stance is to keep cats indoors while in the UK we mainly favour allowing our cats to go outside (most rescue centres will only allow owners to adopt a cat if they have outdoor access).

Most of my behavioural cases are London-based and a good majority involve cats kept solely indoors, so I personally feel cats should be allowed to roam naturally and freely wherever possible and when it's safe for them to do so. Cats should have the opportunity to smell fresh air, hunt naturally (although we can help them be less efficient with their hunting skills by them wearing a bell on a collar, restricting outdoor access at times where their natural prey is out foraging, raising bird feeders out of reach, etc.), guard territory and allowed free choice of movement. When I see people list all of the reasons why a cat should be kept indoors I always change the word 'cat' to 'human'. It is exactly the same (apart from us decimating the local wildlife – although we have actually decimated most things on this earth to near extinction) and yet we wouldn't dream of keeping ourselves, or our children, locked inside for the rest of our/their lives.

Having said this, I am also a big advocate of compromise and will always encourage cat-proofing a garden to keep a cat safe from neighbouring bully cats, main roads or from the ill intentions of humans who wish to do harm to our animals. That way, they get all the benefits of the great outdoors but in a safe way, giving the owner peace of mind. Even window boxes and 'catios' can be built in top-floor flats to ensure a cat can get some fresh air.

The arguments and debates will continue from different groups until the end of time (you'll find lots of debates, some very heated, on the internet), but if a cat owner has a garden, I personally feel it is only fair that the cat gets to enjoy it, too.

Download the free information pack from Mayhew for more information regarding bringing a cat home and letting it outside: www.themayhew.org/wp-content/uploads/2015/04/cat_care.pdf

Find more information online about cat-proofing your garden at protectapet.com

ABOUT THE
AUTHOR

Anita Kelsey BA (Hons), CIDBT, MCFBA is one of a small group of holistic low-stress cat groomers in the UK who are taking cat grooming to the next level. She is the only cat groomer in the UK who also holds a degree in cat behaviour. Anita was awarded a first class honours degree (work-based) in Feline Behaviour and Psychology after graduating from Middlesex University in February 2016. The university also awarded Anita the Gerry Fowler Prize in recognition of her achievement and excellent final result.

Anita is a full member of the Canine and Feline Behaviour Association and is a certified Master Cat Groomer, having studied and trained at a fully operational dog and cat grooming salon in the UK.

Anita's vet-referred behavioural consultation service is dedicated exclusively to the diagnosis and treatment of behavioural problems in cats and she travels all over the UK. The grooming side of her practice concentrates on low-stress handling and Anita is a huge advocate of holistic grooming, which takes into account the mind, body and spirit of each cat as well as the owner in the room. She believes that educating owners is the key to happy matt-free cats. She grooms cats in their own homes in London and is in great demand for her work with the more 'challenging' felines. Her practice also offers hands-on grooming behavioural consultations to owners of cats with issues connected to grooming and is considered to be the first of its kind.

Anita is a features writer for *Your Cat* magazine and is on their experts' panel, giving advice on cat grooming and behaviour. She contributes on a regular basis to the Cats Protection magazine, *The Cat*, and Style Tails, a popular monthly blog. She has written articles for veterinary publications and is regularly interviewed on national radio and in the national press.

Anita is a keen supporter of Mayhew and is a regular volunteer and fundraiser for that charity.

She currently lives in west London with her husband Gordon, a music producer, and their two Norwegian Forest cats, Kiki and Zaza.

Anita can be contacted via her website
www.catbehaviourist.com

For up-to-date cat news and mog tips, please subscribe to Anita's monthly news letter at www.catbehaviourist. com/subscribe, and share your own stories online: #ClawsConfessions